77 Self-Care Treatments

Soul Spa

Spiritual Therapy for Women in Leadership

Joyce A. Mitchell

NEW HOPE
PUBLISHERS

New Hope® Publishers
P. O. Box 12065
Birmingham, AL 35202-2065
www.newhopepublishers.com

New Hope Publishers is a division of WMU®
© 2009 by Joyce A. Mitchell
All rights reserved. First printing 2009.
Printed in the United States of America.

Library of Congress Cataloging-in-Publication Data

Mitchell, Joyce A., 1946-
 Soul spa : spiritual therapy for women in leadership / Joyce A.
Mitchell.
      p. cm. -- (77 self-care devotions)
 Includes bibliographical references and index.
 ISBN-13: 978-1-59669-269-5 (hc : alk. paper)
 ISBN-10: 1-59669-269-3 (hc : alk. paper)
 1. Christian women--Religious life. 2. Leadership--Religious
aspects--Christianity. I. Title.
 BV4527.M5435 2009
 242'.643—dc22
                          2009006127

ISBN-10: 1-59669-269-3
ISBN-13: 978-1-59669-269-5
N094150 • 0609 • 4M1

Dedicated to *Emma Louise Mitchell* who encouraged my first encounter with Christ, and with profound gratitude for Rev. Sarah Jackson Shelton who nurtures fresh encounters with Christ each week.

Contents

Welcome

This book is a plea that the believer create a time to pause and examine her life in terms of how well she is expressing care for herself.

—TREATMENT #2

Welcome to *Soul Spa*, a journey in self-care. An element of our spiritual growth, practicing self-care is a heart-response to God's movement in our lives. Far from being self-indulgent:

> *"Self-care means living the life God has intended for [us]."*
> —*The Spiritual Leader's Guide to Self-Care*

Our Creator God, who connected the distinctive parts of our being—heart, soul, mind, and body—and who made us capable of relating to each other, is surely a wonderful God. And He tells us that we are "fearfully and wonderfully made" (Psalm 139:14 NIV). He intends

7

for us to "love the Lord [our] God with all [our] heart and with all [our] soul and with all [our] mind and with all [our] strength" (Mark 12:30 NIV). Added to this is love for neighbor—relationships (Matthew 22:39 NIV).

No one—other than the individual woman herself—is aware of the state of the interior elements of her life. Each of us, alone, knows whether all is well with our soul.

I personally have not discovered one solution or set of steps that promotes self-care 100 percent of the time, but I do believe developing the habit is a significant start. Experts say it takes 21 to 28 days to develop a new habit (or break an old one). This self-care falls into the category of habits I want to cultivate.

If you are of a similar mind, would you engage in nurturing yourself with these 77 experiences? Allow *Soul Spa* to be your self-care companion. At a pace of one entry per day, you can establish the habit of self-care in your life and for your future.

Step into Your Private *Soul Spa*

For each devotional in the Heart, Soul, Mind, Strength, and Relationships sections, you'll find:

- A proverb or other provocative quote to pique your interest

- A brief reflection, to ponder about some aspect of your self-care

- A journal prompt you may use for musing and journaling

- A random act of self-care you can act on or use as a catalyst to create your own

These can cause us to ponder and plumb tangible as well as intangible benefits of taking time for soul care just as pampering one's physical body produces tangible and intangible benefits. Simply spend a brief time reflecting on what God is stirring in you. These *Soul Spa* moments may serve to spark your creativity and lead you to imagine actions that fit best with who God has made you to be. Add anything you would like, in order to grow in a sense of well-being and happiness.

For example, consider how your self-care can have an impact that you'll share in your relationships.

Soul Spa Experience— Individual and Group Spa Plans

Regarding your relationships, if you decide to embark on this self-care journey with other women, you will find plans for several group approaches, including a retreat plan, on pages 175–83.

Heart

The heart is the very core of a believer's life:
the center or inner part of being.

Empty pockets never held anyone back.
Only empty heads and empty hearts can do that.

—NORMAN VINCENT PEALE

*S*cripture reminds us that the heart is one of several elements of who we are, which includes soul and mind and strength (Mark 12:30). And then Matthew adds: how we relate to others—our neighbors (Matthew 22:39).

These facets of our lives have one thing in common: no one, outside of each one of us, understands or sees the condition of our heart, soul, mind, or strength. Only God, our Creator.

So, each of us should ask our self, *How's my heart today?* Unless you have a heart condition medically, you may not have pondered the state of your heart very much. Here, each day, for the next 16, you'll explore an element of the heart.

A believer's heart is strengthened as she comes to grips with why God has placed her on the planet at this time in history. Engaging God in conversation about life's purpose can be a meaningful experience. Your mind may meander to the movie classic *It's a Wonderful Life.* You may wonder as the main character did: *What if I hadn't been born? What gaps would exist in the lives of my friends, family, and co-workers without me?* That's purpose.

Ponder how satisfied you are with your life as it is today. Wonder how satisfied God is with who you have turned out to be. What do you anticipate for the future? What future dreams require actions today to make the dreams come true? Will lack of resources be an excuse for not pursuing a dream you yearn to fulfill?

> *"The king's heart is in the hand of the Lord;*
> *he directs it like a watercourse wherever he*
> *pleases."*
> —Proverbs 21:1 (NIV)

Today, I'll slow down enough, and sit quietly long enough, to hear what God wants to say.

I won't presume to know the direction of the watercourse God directs.

If He doesn't speak on my schedule, I'll be persistent. I'll ask again. And again.

I'll make a list of nudges God shows to me.

maggie called
essay!
⊙ *mP / workshop*
⊙ *Hoperd email*
⊙ *Resha*

🪨 *Random Act of Self-Care*
Get eight hours of sleep tonight.

Start by doing what is necessary; then do what is
possible; and suddenly you are doing the impossible.

—ST. FRANCIS OF ASSISI

his book is a plea that the believer create a time
to pause and examine her life in terms of how
well she is expressing care for herself.

In the midst of a self-absorbed culture, it would be easy
to veer off the path of reasonable self-care—self-care
that allows one to be her best self in Christ. It would be
easy to make our self the center of our universe.

So much of life is a matter of balance. Balance
between family and profession. Balance between faith
and culture. Balance between our identity in Christ
and our most selfish identities. Balance between work
and play. This list could be expanded by anyone who
thoughtfully reflects on the world in which we live.

How does one balance the words of Jesus in Luke
9:23–25 in which He describes the cost of discipleship
in terms of denying self and following Him, and the
words of the Greatest Commandments in Mark 12:30
and Matthew 22:39?

A very first step in self-care is simply an *intention*
to pay attention. If I find my mind easily hijacked by
the sight of home chores, work projects that require
problem solving, or a demanding church committee,

I am the only one who can carve out a few minutes each day to touch base with myself and ask, *So, self, how are you doing?*

The time frame does not require rising hours earlier than usual, but we must be awake. And if we rely on jotting down our thoughts and heartfelt feelings in a journal, we will have a current journal handy and pen nearby.

When we begin to consider self-care in terms of the Greatest Commandments, a lightbulb should go off in our thinking. The elements of heart, soul, mind, and strength are such an appealing way to look at our inner self.

We can leaf back through earlier entries and see in our own handwriting our efforts to identify the part of self that lacks vision, is obstinate and willful, or lacks generosity. After an aha moment, we can be vigilant about change.

Today, I will pay attention to how I am caring for myself. I may learn something.

Random Act of Self-Care
Sit and listen to the birds.

There are many things in life
that will catch your eye,
but only a few will catch your heart . . . pursue those.

—MICHAEL NOLAN

*T*hink for a moment about those things in life that ignite your passion.

A graphic designer is credited with first using the heart icon in a public relations campaign for New York City: I ♥ NY. This shorthand symbol expresses immediately the warmth and affection that a person feels for a city, sports team, hobby, ethnic food, or another person.

Beyond the people you love, are there ways that you would ideally choose to spend leisure time? Are there recreational or educational pursuits you want to experience; places you'd like to spend time—the beach, the mountains; favorite seasons of the year you'd like to celebrate; exotic locales you want to visit; or creative endeavors that you'd want to do?

What keeps you from indulging yourself in those items on your list?

Sadly, some of us may live our lives without engaging in something we know, or suspect, we love. We may console ourselves with, "When I'm better off financially," or "When I retire," I'll do that.

In a poem, "Warning," the writer announces that

when she's an old woman, she will wear purple, and a red hat that doesn't go with anything, and engage in several activities she has always wanted to do. But the last lines of the poem indicate she thinks maybe she better not wait till she's an old woman. She's going to try some of those things now!

Today, I will reflect on activities or pursuits that I would like to cultivate.

My list may be short because I'm out of practice of imagining *what if.*

My goal will be to surface just ten things that ignite my heart.

And I'll ponder what it would take to make one of these a reality this year!

🔺 *Random Act of Self-Care*
Invite several friends to my home for a sleepover.

Everyone is kneaded out of the same dough
but not baked in the same oven.

—YIDDISH PROVERB

*L*ife purpose is the bedrock of who you are.

Our purpose as individuals determines where we are
headed in life.

Consider the roles you play. Several are seren-
dipitous: biological or adopted family, cultural lineage,
regional heritage, DNA pool, familial relationships, and
so on. These are given to you.

Other life roles give us an opportunity to decide: the
profession pursued, the schools we enroll in, and the
marital status we choose. Roles are more diverse than a
first glance would indicate: think of friendships, volunteer opportunities woven into a schedule, citizenship,
and learning pursuits.

Roles can be natural and good fits. This happens
when our gifts and skills are allowed to flourish. Other
roles are a stretch. A workplace consultant has observed
that more than 75 percent of employees are hired into
positions that are not good matches for their skills. He
suggested that working in a job that is not a good fit is
like walking around all day, carrying a folding chair under
your arm. Fatigue is bound to set in by the day's end.

God reassures us that the Master Designer is in charge of our being.

> *"You know me inside and out, you know*
> *every bone in my body; You know exactly*
> *how I was made, bit by bit, how I was*
> *sculpted from nothing into something."*
> —PSALM 139:15 (*The Message*)

One of the mysteries of being God's creation is that He makes our hearts glad when we choose to live out a role He has created for us. He is pleased when we say yes to a challenge or opportunity that uniquely fits us.

Today, I'll explore the roles in life that give me a sense of nearness and obedience to God.

I'll make a list of the roles that are draining and might well fit someone else.

I'll be grateful for God's wisdom in discerning the roles I might shed and the new roles He's leading me into. This day may hold surprises!

🪨 *Random Act of Self-Care*
Share vacation pictures with a friend.

Your absence has gone through me
Like thread through a needle.
Everything I do is stitched with its color.

—W. S. MERWIN

*R*elationships are critical elements within our
lives.

Think about individuals who were once a part of your
life and are now absent. Who do you miss the most?

As young children, we form all sorts of friendships—
people our age, even adults, and maybe animals. Some
friends are even imaginary. At the time, we believe these
friends will be a part of our lives forever. Then families
move. Or a friend develops a passion for cheerleading,
and we're not cheerleader material.

As adults, we become increasingly acquainted with
the pain of adult separations through divorce or disagree-
ments, through death, through lives that drift apart.

What do you recall about your earliest friendships?
Perhaps you were a loner, spending time with books or
music or art or creative writing.

Down the street from my childhood home lived a
noisy, rambunctious family who had eight children.
Slipping into my bed each night in a room I shared with
my only sister, I wondered what it would be like to have
seven siblings. I imagined bliss! The reality might have

been closer to frustration as I had to learn lessons about how to share and take my turn.

Our lives are a crazy quilt stitched by the friendships and relationships with which God has blessed us. The kind of friend you are today may reflect a lesson you learned from a childhood friend.

Primary in our circle of friendships is our ongoing relationship with God, our loving Father. God may not appear to us, as He did to Moses, in a pillar of cloud at the entrance to the tent of meeting. God may not choose to speak to us, as he did to Moses, face-to-face, "as a man speaks with his friend" (Exodus 33:11 NIV). Yet, far from being separate from us, God is available for daily communion with His children.

How do you nurture your relationship with God? How do you allow Him to speak to you as a friend?

Today, I'll think about the relationships God has stitched into my life. They are by His design.

I'll be grateful because of those influences and for friends who have left their legacy as well.

I'll reconnect with someone with whom I've lost touch: a call, an email, or a letter.

I'll also make it a point to communicate with my heavenly Father today.

🔺 *Random Act of Self-Care*
Begin keeping a file of affirming letters, cards, and email messages, and reread them periodically.

Truth strikes us from behind, and in the dark.
—HENRY DAVID THOREAU

*C*ommunication with God, others, and self are essential elements of a believer's daily life.

It is frustrating to misunderstand or to be misunderstood by others. Yet it happens more frequently than we would like.

A valuable tool in safeguarding against misunderstanding is simply to listen. Listen to what God is saying. Pause to really hear the words from those vying for our attention. Pose a clarifying question to dig more deeply into what the words might mean.

Listening requires that we turn off or turn down our internal monologue so that we can pay attention to the one talking to us. We may be the only one who is willing to listen to this person. We listen, not to solve, or fix, or advise, or (heaven forbid) to one-up his or her story. We listen simply to provide a time and a person who deems his or her story worth hearing.

Someone has observed, "Listening is more than waiting for my turn to talk."

The psalmist pleads eloquently that God would:

> *"Give ear to my words . . . give heed to my sighing. Listen to the sound of my cry. . . .*

*O Lord, in the morning you hear my voice;
in the morning I plead my case to you, and
watch."*

—PSALM 5:1–3 (NRSV)

Journal keepers have a natural mechanism for tracking their internal conversations. They need only look at entries from years past to see the issues that consumed their attention, the concerns that weighed them down, their fears, their worries, and what they were celebrating.

For those who include written prayers as part of their journaling, dependence on the power of memory or recollection is minimal.

Today, I will think more deeply about a few of the communications that are a part of my life.

Do I allow God the space in my life to reveal those things He wants me to know, to act on, and to make a part of my life?

How approachable and trustworthy do others view me?

In whom do I most often confide? Who turns to me as a listening ear?

🪨 *Random Act of Self-Care*

Have a tea party with friends younger than ten years old.

Faith is a journey . . . without maps.

—FREDERICK BUECHNER

A key process for the believer is the faith journey.

And what can the believer expect in terms of directions or a map on this sort of journey?

I like maps, step-by-step instructions, recipes, and models to follow! There's a certain comfort in knowing that, by following a path tested by others, I am likely to succeed.

Companions for the living out of faith, day to day, surely include the written Word of God—the Bible—and communication with God—prayer. God's Spirit abides with us and is instrumental in prompting us to act in ways that may seem, on reflection, inexplicable such as noticing something, or feeling the urge to pray, or the impulse to speak to someone. A friend of mine describes these impulses as "God sending an angel to enliven me."

The experiences of those who have journeyed before us can shed great light for us, particularly in written accounts describing their adventures. And those circles of people whose lives intersect with ours often impart real-life words of wisdom, encouragement, insight, and comfort—at just the right time.

We often do not grasp the ultimate direction or destination to which God is leading us on our faith journey. Our experience with God tells us He is faithful to lead us. We have sufficient light for today. And that is enough.

Today, I will pause to think about the light that God has been faithful to provide in my life.

My life has not been frozen in time. I have moved since yesterday, and last year, and five years ago. Who is setting the pace and leading the way?

In what personal life experience might I have lost sight of God's map? What can I learn from that departure?

How can I rediscover God's path?

Random Act of Self-Care
Visit the old neighborhood.

> Above all else, guard your heart,
> for it is the wellspring of life.
>
> —PROVERBS 4:23 (NIV)

*H*ow would you describe the issues that concern you?

A five-year-old friend was busy with several toys on his family room floor. Nearby, his work-at-home mom focused on her laptop computer. Sam requested his mother's attention by repeating, "Mom. Mom. Mom."

His mother responded, but her eyes stayed on her computer screen, "What do you need?"

He demanded again, "Mom. Mom. I've got issues."

At that, she turned to look squarely at her son. "What? You're playing!"

Satisfied that she was fully attentive, he informed her, "I've got puzzle issues."

The issues that might give us a sleepless night may range from a challenging personal decision, a relationship, stress from the job, financial uncertainty, demands from family or friends, a personal goal that's off track, and more. Following global or local news with any regularity may cause anxiety about world events such as war, drought, or financial or other crisis.

Even anticipatory, happy issues—excitement about an upcoming vacation, the purchase of a first house, an approaching wedding—can bring some anxiety. Issues are issues. And often they deflect us from paying attention to life in real time.

> *"Don't fret or worry. Instead of worrying, pray. Let petitions and praises shape your worries into prayers, letting God know your concerns. Before you know it, a sense of God's wholeness, everything coming together for good, will come and settle you down. It's wonderful what happens when Christ displaces worry at the center of your life."*
>
> —PHILIPPIANS 4:6–7 (*The Message*)

What would it take for you to release your life issues—the problems you anticipate, big and small—into God's hands? Wouldn't your step be lighter and your mood cheerier if you were unencumbered with worries?

Today, I will literally bring to mind my top ten issues, writing them down.

I'll place the list in an envelope, seal it, and date it.

In a month, I'll repeat the exercise and see if my issues are the same.

🪨 *Random Act of Self-Care*
Learn to crochet, knit, or tat.

Change your thoughts
and you change the world.
—NORMAN VINCENT PEALE

The practice of hospitality is a habit that enriches the hearts of both the host and the guest.

Do you know someone hospitable? I have fond memories of a pastor's wife who rose early on Sunday mornings to prepare a great Sunday dinner feast. Effie's joy was to invite church members and visitors alike home to dine with her family. Guests helped set the table and clean up afterward. Gratitude for the food and fellowship launched the meal. Laughter, stories, and concerns punctuated the bites of the fine dinner she prepared.

While away at school, I recall a host family in my church who adopted seminary students. We were always grateful for being included at various times in their family lives. That was genuine hospitality. Hearts were warmed because of the graciousness of the host family.

In professional life, I have learned that an invitation to friends and co-workers to share a simple dinner (I may joke that it might only be "a can of pork and beans") is always greeted with gratitude. Generally, it's a more elaborate menu than a can of beans, which causes even more gratitude.

Romans 12:13 (CEV) reminds us to "take care of God's needy people and welcome strangers into your home."

Ponder this: *Where have I learned my philosophy of hospitality?*

Believers' hearts are enriched by welcoming friends and family to our tables. Even if the tables are TV tables, or a card table, and the menu is carryout from the nearby restaurant.

An elderly church friend used to bring several brown bags to church on Sunday. She would give a loaf of homemade bread to church friends, usually different people, each Sunday. As the recipient of a loaf of her bread, I felt honored and blessed. That's hospitality, Miss Marion-style. And this warmed my heart.

Today, I will reflect on the hospitality of others that has been bestowed on me.

I'll ponder what unique gifts I might offer to those with whom my life intersects—a neighbor, a co-worker, an old or new friend, a family member, even a stranger.

 Random Act of Self-Care

Invite a neighbor to tour the local botanical gardens together.

Forgive one another as quickly and thoroughly
as God in Christ forgave you.

—EPHESIANS 4:32 (*The Message*)

*W*hen someone close to us says something or
acts in a way that causes us pain, the healthiest
response is to be forgiving.

It takes energy to hold a grudge, harbor resentment,
or nurse a wound. How energizing to offer the gift of
forgiveness and get on with life.

Forgiveness is easiest when it is practiced regularly.
How do we know when it's time to forgive? One surefire
test is to recall what makes us angry.

The marriage of a friend ended suddenly. Whenever
she was with friends and acquaintances, the topic
became a litany of hurts she had experienced in her
failed marriage. Over a period of time, the mistakes of
her spouse became old news and a stale rerun for her
friends and family.

But she could not let the hurt go. She was angry, and
the failure of this relationship consumed her. Friends
and even some family members began to avoid her.
Until she sought counseling help, the network of those
who were willing to befriend her kept shrinking.

A decision to forgive another person often requires
a day-by-day commitment to continue forgiving.

This friend resolved to be intentional about trying to practice forgiveness once she discerned the impact that her bitterness toward her former spouse was having on others. She began to involve herself in activities that gave her fresh topics of conversation to have with friends. She did not have to rely on the default topic of "husband-bashing."

One of her aha moments was that *she* needed the benefit of forgiving her former spouse. (He had never asked for forgiveness, nor was he likely to do so.) She imagined a moment in the future when she would encounter a new friend or co-worker who might express surprise, "Oh, I didn't realize you were divorced."

She's looking forward to that future day.

Today, I will explore my circle of friends and family, past and present. Who stands in need of my forgiveness? If I can reconnect with that person, I will do so.

How will I express understanding, empathy, or compassion for someone who has hurt me?

Do I have the courage to explore old hurts?

Is there someone who needs to hear me say, "I'm sorry. Will you forgive me?"

🪨 *Random Act of Self-Care*

Go to the zoo and watch people and animals.

Gratitude is not only
the greatest of virtues,
but the parent of all the others.

—CICERO

*I*t is impossible to create an exhaustive list of the benefits of a grateful heart.

I attended a meeting once in which a thoughtful pray-er opened with these words:

"Thank You, God, for this day, a day like no other day we have ever experienced. A day that, once gone, can never be repeated."

I don't recall anything he said following his initial observation. I was taken with the thought that, indeed, the day was a unique gift. And my mind raced on to imagine, how would *I* observe or commemorate this day? How would I give attention to life during this day that was beginning to unfold? How would the day conclude?

Every day has this same potential. Discovering the unique and memorable aspects of the day requires a sense of anticipation on the part of a believer. A sense of expectancy. A willingness to even look back at the day with the thoughtfulness of a grateful heart.

Psychologists attribute any number of positive behavioral characteristics to simply being grateful.

They note that grateful people are likely to be more alert, enthusiastic, determined, optimistic, and energetic.

It would seem that there is deep truth in the gospel hymn, "Count Your Blessings." One popular media hostess has touted the benefit of keeping a gratitude journal. After interviewing Sarah Ban Breathnach, author of *Simple Abundance*, conversation about gratitude journals began to escalate on the Internet as well as within personal conversations.

Gratitude becomes more than a habit we dust off at Thanksgiving. It becomes a practice we engage in every day.

Today, I will act in such a way that others will be grateful that I held an elevator for them or offered a word of encouragement or shared a solution to a dilemma.

I will be mindful of those gifts of my Creator that enliven my day—an azalea in full, riotous bloom; a warm welcome from my pet; or a homemade cookie from a friend.

Random Act of Self-Care
Light a favorite aromatic candle.

Journal writing is a voyage to the interior.

—CHRISTINA BALDWIN

*J*ournaling is simply a tool to get in touch with the inner thinking that everyone does.

It is easy to become self-conscious when writing a journal entry. A person might think: *Who am I that I think my thoughts are so important or deep that they are worth collecting? My thoughts may be only important for an audience of one: me.*

Not everyone chooses to write out daily what they are thinking, of course.

However, one benefit of keeping a journal is that the journal keeper makes the rules . . . or dispenses with them. Daily entries? Length of entries? Bound journal or loose-leaf paper? Portable journal or computer entries? Write in the morning or evening? The options are endless. And habit and patterns shift through the years.

Three questions that offer an intriguing tool in journaling; they are deceptively simple:

What surprised me?

What touched me?

What inspired me?

Framing thoughts about the previous hours of life fit very well with this trio of questions—or only one of them. Perhaps the previous day was full of surprises and a space of time can involve exploring those surprises. Other days, the journal keeper might respond to each of the questions.

Mornings—or evenings—journaling may springboard from reading Scripture and devotional books; jotting down a Scripture passage, a quote, or a phrase from a book that impresses. A journal can be an eclectic hodgepodge of prayer concerns, and our ongoing dialogue with God about those issues that are of deepest concern. That is one journal style. Ask yourself, *What kind of journaler am I?*

Today, I will experiment with the trio of questions in my journal. I may learn something new!

🔺 *Random Act of Self-Care*
Write with a fountain pen.

You may go where you wish,
but you cannot escape yourself.

—NORWEGIAN PROVERB

*W*hat does collecting (or not collecting) say about you?

You may know individuals dedicated to collecting something. They may favor figurines, shoes, dolls, pottery, or baseball caps. They may collect items based on a theme, like roosters, cows, lighthouses, angels, or Christmas nativities.

What do you collect? If you were to consciously observe, do you lean toward a certain type of books on your bookshelves: Southern fiction, books on prayer, Civil War history, children's literature, or poetry? That's a collection.

At times, it's a reality check to notice that other people favor something other than what we collect, if they collect at all. Because I read and collect cookbooks, it took me a while to realize that not all of my friends and family shared my preferences. Finally, a friend hinted that she didn't have room for one more cookbook. I took the remark to heart. No more cookbooks for her!

Do you find yourself energized when you're around fellow collectors? Have you considered what will happen to your collection when you change your living space, or move on? Most individuals who care enough to search, gather, and collect have thought about a person who would appreciate their collections.

The organization where I serve has received gifts of numerous collections from missionaries. Collections of dolls, personal letters, indigenous art, native costumes, photographs, and more, make their way to our building. Memorabilia displays enhance our lobby and hallways because missionaries have given us the privilege of receiving their collections, and telling their stories.

It's never too late to start a collection, but I suspect if you look carefully at your living space, you may discover you already have.

Today, I'll reflect on what I collect, or I might begin to collect.

I'll consider that a collection may be material items, or as simple as collecting and recording intriguing names or unusual words.

I'll pay attention to what I and others collect and think about what each of these collections say about us.

🪨 *Random Act of Self-Care*
Sit on a park bench for at least 15 minutes.

All I have seen teaches me
to trust the creator
for all I have not seen.
—RALPH WALDO EMERSON

*C*onsider where you learned valuable life lessons.

Chances are you learned valuable life lessons by experience as well as observation. You learned them from your parents, your teachers, and friends. You may have learned several from failures in life, as well as from successes.

As a kindergartner, I accompanied my grandfather to a neighborhood market. Though I could barely see the countertop, I did observe the candy display at my eye level. I selected a favorite candy bar and slipped it into my pocket.

On the walk home, I proudly showed the candy to my grandfather. A tall man, he knelt to my eye level and explained why I couldn't keep it. And, we walked back to the store, where I returned the candy and apologized for taking something that wasn't mine. I was embarrassed, and, especially because I sensed that I had disappointed my grandfather, I never stole again.

Robert Fulghum declares that he learned everything he needed to know in kindergarten, in his similarly titled book. Most of us are still learning lessons every day of our lives.

An aunt would visit our family, and immediately after eating dinner, would retreat to lie down on a sofa and announce that her head was "swimming." Meantime, my mother, sister, and I would clear the table and clean the kitchen. Miraculously, her head returned to a nonswimming state about the time we finished. The lesson? Adults can be conveniently sick, just like kids.

Think of lessons that are clearly planted in your mind and heart. It is also good to recall that we influence others by the lessons we impart. What have you learned? And what are you teaching others?

Today, I will reflect and note at least a half dozen lessons I have learned so far.

I'll let my mind drift back to the time in life when I learned each of those lessons. Who taught me? What was the situation?

I'll think also of a recent lesson that is fresh in my mind.

Random Act of Self-Care
Research the ideal vacation on the Internet.

The unexamined life
is not worth living.

—SOCRATES

*O*rdinary circumstances can be the source of rich nuggets of life—wisdom.

Discerning what is wisdom requires that we be fully present with family, friends, co-workers, and others, as well as pay attention to life unfolding around us.

Journals are a handy and natural spot to store wise sayings, quotations, book titles, and so on. We can cull and note the wisdom from events we experience. The only prerequisite is that we pay attention.

At a birthday party of a young friend, his older four-year-old sister was reprimanded firmly by her mother. Sarah's misbehavior was simply being too active a helper to her younger brother. She was obscuring her mother's view, while Mother tried to videotape the birthday boy unwrapping his gifts.

Mother's impatient admonishment had an immediate impact on Sarah. Her face collapsed in sorrow, tears sprung from her eyes, and she fled to the comforting arms of a nearby aunt. Her lament contained such remorse, "Was I wrong? Was I really wrong?" that, though I smiled at the time, I recall the pathos in her voice to this day.

How much better adult relationships would be if we had the same degree of remorse that Sarah had whenever we acted or spoke harmfully to another person. If we walk through recent days, have we inadvertently stepped on someone's toes? Cut off another's contribution? Blocked a friend's desire to share? Talked over, or interrupted a slower-tongued colleague?

My co-worker Caroline and I have different styles of creativity. She thinks aloud, and often at length. I try to listen attentively, but am often guilty of summing up what she's saying before she's finished saying it. Her body language quickly tells me when I've overstepped, and I need to give her more thinking-aloud time. I need to assure Caroline that I value her thinking and am not trying to stifle her creativity.

Today, I will be present with those individuals who are participants in my life.

I'll review our conversations mentally, and when I find myself being the obstacle, I'll act to make it right.

Random Act of Self-Care

Listen to a child tell a story.

Write it on your heart that every day
is the best day in the year.

—RALPH WALDO EMERSON

*H*ow do I deal with a day in which events don't quite go my way?

A young friend Alyssa came home from preschool minus her usual animated and happy smile. In response to a few questions from her mother, she replied, "I didn't get a star today." This was Alyssa's first experience with not receiving a star. She kept printing several of her alphabet letters backwards.

Alyssa's mother quickly assured her that everyone makes mistakes in printing when they first begin and reminded her of many earlier stars. The preschooler's sad face remained unchanged. Before her mother could offer any additional comfort, Alyssa wisely counseled her mother, "Mom, you don't get it. You either get a star, or you don't."

In spite of her age, Alyssa grasped that failing to measure up happens. And no loving words from Mom were going to replace the star she didn't receive at preschool. But, she would go back to preschool tomorrow and try to earn a star. She was practical and matter-of-fact.

Maybe you had a different, and possibly unrealistic, vision for the outcome of a project or a conversation. You possibly underestimated the difficulty of finding a solution.

Someone has observed that unrealized expectations are often among the deepest disappointments we experience. When our dreams, desires, and needs lead us to expect a "star," and we come home without one, we are inevitably discouraged.

We have a choice. Some people expect the worst so they won't be disappointed with the outcome. That stance is too negative for others who would rather be hopefully optimistic. Optimistic people are the ones we most enjoy being around! What about you?

Today, I will inventory how I'm doing in noticing the events of life that inspire or touch me. These are "stars" I'll cherish, as are those people or experiences that bring the element of surprise into my life.

How have I been surprised in the past 24 hours?

🪨 *Random Act of Self-Care*
Take a canoe trip or a ferryboat ride.

Soul

Of utmost concern to God is how we are.

—TREATMENT #20

A mile walked with a friend contains
only a hundred steps.

—RUSSIAN PROVERB

$\mathcal{S}$ome friendships are soul friendships. How can you tell?

Author Debra Farrington notes in *Hearing with the Heart*, "We need to surround ourselves with those who can help us discern and stay on the path, . . . who can encourage us and . . . be our champions."

Imagine a collage composed simply of photographs of faces. Faces of all the people who you have ever called friend. What a masterpiece! Your memory may be stretched to recall the actual names of these people. You likely have lost contact with a few. Life intervenes. Geography creates barriers. Careers and families cause our paths to diverge.

One observer has commented that we have friends of the road and friends of the heart. Friends who travel the road with us may fade when that stretch of the journey is complete: college, a professional assignment, or even life in a neighborhood. Those friendships are real and have substance—for a time. The friendship is simply transitory.

Friends of the heart are a longer-lasting variety of relationship. In addition to shared experiences, weathering life crises, these individuals really get the essence of who we are. Months and miles may intervene, but the reunions are heartfelt. It is as if a magnetic force field binds friends of the heart together. Efforts are made to keep the connection alive, maybe not the day-to-day details but significant elements of each others' lives.

Both types of friends feed our souls. We cherish those with whom we can be transparent, those who care for us and to whom we reciprocate care, and those who are loyal to us, as we are to them.

Jesus reminds us in John 15:15 (NIV), "I have called you friends." As we befriend each other, we gather in communities of faith and "learn to be friends to each other" as Fisher Humphreys says in his book, *I Have Called You Friends.* Consider the variety of friendships that are emerging between you and those who worship at your side.

Today, I'll make it a point to take time to genuinely listen to a friend.

I'll pose a question or two and give my friend the opportunity to respond.

I'll try to stifle my impulse to give advice.

I'll journal a prayer for a friend whose life circumstance stands in need of prayer.

🔺 *Random Act of Self-Care*

Take a Sunday afternoon nap.

> Then the Lord put out his hand
> and touched my mouth; and the Lord said to me,
> "Now I have put my words in your mouth."
>
> —JEREMIAH 1:9 (NRSV)

*W*hat's your faith story?

I recall a Sunday School teacher, Mr. Bryan, guiding our class through an exercise in which we wrote our testimony on a 3-by-5 note card. He said the discipline would help us be focused and clear when we had the opportunity to tell another person about our relationship with Jesus Christ.

He challenged us by asking us to imagine riding on an elevator and having to tell another passenger our testimony by the time the elevator arrived at the top floor and the doors opened.

Being a person of many words, I struggled with the exercise. I had so many details that I wanted to fit on the card. Many cards later, I finally was able to reduce the story of what my life was like before I became a believer, how I recognized my need of Christ, and what my life was like once I accepted Christ.

I have had many opportunities to share my faith story since then. None was more unexpected than a visit I made while traveling with a friend. She asked if we had time to stop and visit her uncle in a nearby town. We found his home, and he greeted us warmly. He even served us iced tea. No sooner than we had our beverage, this wizened older man turned a kindly face toward me and inquired about my conversion story. He told me he collected conversion stories and wanted to know mine. (He already knew his niece was a Christian.)

I wasn't expecting to be asked, but I certainly had a story to share with him. He smiled when I finished and told me that he'd found this approach worked real well with listeners. Because, if anyone was unable to tell a conversion story, then he'd share from his Bible and show them the way.

I've thought of the practicality and effectiveness of this church deacon's practice many times since.

Today, I will record a simple, straightforward, and short version of how my life was changed by meeting Jesus Christ.

Random Act of Self-Care

Share something with a friend that has surprised, touched, or inspired me.

> Years wrinkle the skin, but to give up
> enthusiasm wrinkles the soul.
>
> —DOUGLAS MACARTHUR

*M*y friend stands out because of her simple approach toward others.

Ruth comes from a background in early childhood education. In any adult gathering, she smiles engagingly, introduces herself, and immediately opens the door for people to tell about themselves—their day, their family, what brought them to the event, and so on. Often, she simply compliments them on something they're wearing—a piece of jewelry, sweater, or something else. But she always follows up with the invitation to tell the story of how they came to possess the item. She seldom breaks eye contact.

She has a most endearing characteristic: she is interested in other people. Nearly always, people are warmed by her interest and willingly share all manner of information about themselves. People often describe Ruth as easy to talk to.

There's no deep mystery about why they draw that conclusion: she practices the gracious gift of interest: genuine interest and undivided attention.

Contrast Ruth with three acquaintances whose conversational approaches leave a lot to be desired.

First person: often monopolizes lunch-table conversation. Seldom does anyone else have an opportunity to say much because she keeps up a steady monologue: what's happening in her family, her church, her life, what she's watching on TV, and more.

Second person: always has the most heartrending and sad stories to share. Often these events are true accounts from her family, but she seems to collect items from current news, if the details are dire enough.

Third person: has adopted a refrain of lament that usually grinds conversation to a halt—"The problem is . . ." she announces. As you might suspect, she sees everything in terms of its problematic nature.

Ruth, however, consistently focuses on the other person. People gravitate toward her because of her winsome habit of expressing interest in their lives. I suspect that my three acquaintances are unaware of the impact of their conversational styles.

Today, I will listen to myself, as well as others.

Am I making it easy for others to share concerns of their hearts?

Do I disclose appropriately?

Who are the top three people with whom I enjoy conversation? Whose list of conversational favorites am I on?

Random Act of Self-Care
Invite friends over for a game night.

Faith is the daring of the soul to go
farther than it can see.

—WILLIAM NEWTON CLARKE

*T*he path to strengthening our souls involves abiding in the presence of our Father.

My sister Donna and I enrolled in an elementary school located nearly eight blocks from our home. Mother walked my sister to school during her first week as a kindergartner. The city schoolyard was bustling with children waiting for the school door to be unlocked. Mother and Donna arrived. Clutching Mother's hand nervously, Donna observed the noisy crowd of energetic and playful schoolmates. Her eyes welled with tears at the thought of saying good-bye to Mother.

Mother reassured her, "Don't forget, honey, I'll be back to pick you up at lunchtime." Donna's voice quavered as she surveyed the playground once more, "Mom, how will you know my face?"

Mother promised Donna she wouldn't forget her face.

It is comforting to consider that God intimately knows not only our faces. He is also familiar with what's going on in our minds, and in our hearts, and in our souls. He created us, after all. We are His children.

Of utmost concern to God is how we are. Are we living the kinds of lives that are meaningful and making a difference in the world? Do we demonstrate a genuine sense of joy because of the relationship we have with God, our heavenly Father? Are we seeking growth experiences that stretch us as missional believers who serve God?

Just as there was certainty that Mother would never forget Donna's one-of-a-kind face, we can experience a certainty that God will never forget or forsake us. His written Word contains promises that elaborate on the love God has for His Creation.

Today, I'll spend some time reflecting on Scripture that reminds me of the unique relationship God had in mind when He created me.

I'll record favorite verses and marvel at the invitation God has provided for abundant life.

I'll enjoy simply being in His presence.

Random Act of Self-Care

Take a walk in the rain, or sunshine, or, if there's snow, make a snow angel.

Laughter is the spark of the soul.

—ANONYMOUS

SOUL

*L*aughter is good for the soul.

When we laugh, scientists tell us, a chemical called serotonin is released into our brains. The result? This feel-good hormone gives us a sense of well-being and optimism. Regardless of our life circumstances.

A friend was in the midst of complaining about several issues that were plaguing her life. "Every time I turn around," she announced, "the house needs to be repaired, or my car is on the fritz, or I have a new ache or pain." An observer, who possessed great childlike wisdom, advised, "Quit turning 'round."

Do you find opportunities every day for a healthy dose of laughter? Self-deprecating laughter is often the best of all: when we stop taking ourselves so seriously, step back, and enjoy a situation in which we might be a key player.

At one time, parking space was scarce near my downtown apartment. The alley behind the building provided the best spots. I was frustrated one morning to see that, because I had pulled very close to a telephone pole, I could not open the passenger-side door. Not an issue except another car now was inches away from my driver's door. I was, naturally, running late that morning.

The close conditions allowed barely enough room for me to squeeze my long arm in to open the window. After which I hoisted myself into the car through the window opening. Midway through this contortion, the thought struck me that the upper-story apartment dwellers had a clear view of my awkward maneuvering with legs flutter-kicking madly. Laughter overtook me.

My soul was nurtured that morning because of a hearty (and humbling) dose of laughter at my own expense. The day was punctuated with a memory of how I had managed to enter my car, and gratitude that this wasn't a regular habit!

Today, I'll look for opportunities to harvest the humor in my life.

When have I been able to laugh at myself?

When do I wish that I had exercised laughter instead of another emotion such as anger or frustration?

🔺 *Random Act of Self-Care*

Make a batch of jelly or jam or preserves.

Remember that you were a slave in the land of Egypt, and the Lord your God brought you out from there by a mighty hand and by an outstretched arm; therefore the Lord your God commanded you to keep the Sabbath day.

*I*n previous generations, and especially in small towns, keeping Sabbath was the norm.

Blue laws enforced moral standards, particularly the observance of Sunday as a day of worship or rest. Commerce and amusement were carefully regulated. Stores were closed and shopping ceased. Today, many of these laws have been repealed or declared unconstitutional or are simply unenforced.

Dorothy C. Bass notes in *Practicing Our Faith*, "Sabbath keeping is not about taking a day off but about being recalled to our knowledge of and gratitude for God's activity in creating the world, giving liberty to captives, and overcoming the powers of death."

In order for the soul to be nurtured through a day of rest, the individual must be intentional about framing the day as one of a different rhythm and pace. Sunday afternoons may be that unusual time when a nap is the best way to honor our bodies and God. Being intentional about not postponing every manner of chores to complete on Sunday is a discipline. Even our communities of faith that frequently schedule committee meetings for Sundays can select a different day.

Keeping Sabbath may include a nature or neighborhood walk or an unprecedented time for spiritual reading or praying. It may include a gathering of friends or family with whom we share and by whom we are nurtured.

Hebrews 4:10 (CEV) reminds us that "on that day God's people will rest from their work, just as God rested from his work."

Today, I will reflect on the meaning of the statement that nothing about my life is hidden from God. Am I comforted by this thought, or am I uneasy? Why?

I will ponder my life to this date and recall the instances in which I have heard God clearly speak to my soul; those instances are memory.

And I will imagine those issues in my life about which I need to hear a word from God. Because He has been faithful, I will trust, resting in the truth that I will receive a word again, in God's timing.

Random Act of Self-Care
Wear a hat to church.

If of thy mortal goods thou art bereft,
And from thy slender store
Two loaves alone to thee are left,
Sell one and from the dole,
Buy Hyacinths to feed the soul.

—MUSLIH-UDDIN SADI

*D*o you imagine from time to time exactly what it is that feeds your soul?

You may not reflect on this much; possibly you're too busy. Maybe a tea party with family and friends would feed your soul. Or watching a magnificent sunset. Or finishing a 5K race. Or quiet moments in conversation with God, alone.

I enjoy entertaining. And I thoroughly enjoy the presence of guests in my home. But I also relish the time before the first friend arrives. My home is spic-and-span for company. Aromas of a favorite food waft from my kitchen. I survey the house, my mind racing with anticipation of friends' arrival. This solitary time stirs within me a sense of profound gratitude for the blessings of home, hearth, and friends. The anticipation of their visit nurtures my soul.

What keeps us from feeding our souls with intentionality and regularity? A co-worker suggested a theme for an upcoming event: Fast Lives, Quiet Hearts.

I identified with the spirit of that theme. Another friend suggested Battered by Busyness as a theme for her hectic life.

Many of us have biblical Martha-like tendencies, indelibly imprinted in our DNA. Dare we take time from our home, our families, our careers, to nurture our souls?

Today, I'll think about how I might fill in these blanks with responses that fit me.

If I had the time, I would like to learn _____ _____ .

If I had the money, I would like to explore

_____ .

If I had time and money, I would like to experience_____ .

What would I have to do to indulge myself in one of these soul-nurturing activities?

🗂 *Random Act of Self-Care*

Play a game with a child (such as Uno, Candyland, or Go Fish).

> Pray often; for prayer is a shield to the soul, a
> sacrifice to God, and a scourge for Satan.
>
> —JOHN BUNYAN

*P*rayer experiences underscore the importance of the practice of prayer.

I recall intense and lively dialogues with friends about the real intent of Paul's word that we "pray without ceasing" (1 Thessalonians 5:17 NRSV). How was that possible? What was the spirit of the Apostle Paul's words? What was the application to our young collegiate lives? Were we not to sleep? Or attend classes? Only pray?

Pray whether I am in the mood to pray—or not. Whether the answers I request are delivered—or not. Whether I think I have the time to pray—or not.

Our commitment to pray is strengthened when we remember that God has been faithful throughout our lives. Our relationship rests on the regular conversation we have together. When a circumstance arises that is beyond us, we must turn to God.

The memory I have of "peeking" during a prayertime as a youth and observing the face of Brother Richardson praying is etched in my mind. In simple words, with his head bowed, he implored God on behalf of the concerns of our family of faith. He had no written prayer. He prayed by heart. As a very young believer, I determined

I wanted to have that kind of familiarity with prayer too. And especially, I wanted the kind of relationship with God that made praying genuine.

Praying without ceasing also includes an element of persistence. Not that God needs us to remind Him of some current devastation, for example. But if we are to be instruments of God's love in a cyclone-ravaged country, or in a crime-ridden community, or in a conflict-plagued context, we must keep the lines of communication open to God, allowing Him to prompt us—expecting Him to prompt us.

Today, I will write a prayer in my journal. I'll express gratitude for the privilege of prayer, of being heard and accepted by a loving Creator God.

I'll record a few of the prayer lessons that occur to me.

And I'll express my willingness to grow in the practice of prayer, for my soul's sake.

Random Act of Self-Care
Go to the beach and watch the waves or to the park and watch wind sway the trees.

On the day I called, You answered me;
You made me bold with strength in my soul.

—PSALM 138:3 (NASB)

SOUL

𝓛earning and growing in prayer is a worthwhile interest.

When I read about a silent retreat at a nearby convent, I signed up to attend. I had my initial immersion experience into contemplative—also known as centering—prayer.

The accommodations were simple, plain rooms in the convent. The food was cafeteria-style and plentiful. We had an opportunity to attend a Catholic mass, which was a first for me. The rule of maintaining silence was the most jarring, since I was attending with several women from my church and yearned to chat with them about what we were experiencing.

The opportunity to learn about the contemplative prayer tradition from several leaders, who happened to be Catholic women, was insightful. To engage in this prayer with a small group who represented multiple faith traditions was a good reminder of the unity God desires believers to have in Christ. To be led to practice the prayer technique was a rich experience as well. For someone whose major engagements in prayer were extemporaneous and verbal, either personally or in corporate worship, this reflective and silent type of approach was quite a contrast.

I find benefits in slowing down, breathing deeply, observing silence, and waiting for God to speak to me.

Today, I will reflect on the prayer practices that most enrich my life.

I'll consider how I have grown in prayer and how praying nurtures my soul.

I'll think about changes to my prayer life and what keeps me from exploring those changes.

Random Act of Self-Care

Enjoy a few sprigs of lilac, forsythia, or cherry blossoms.

Beautiful music is the art of the prophets that can calm the agitations of the soul; it is one of the most magnificent and delightful presents God has given us.

—MARTIN LUTHER

*L*isten. What do you hear that restores your soul?

Sometimes, being utterly silent can be a welcome relief. It may be rare to find a moment during the day that is not full of noise generated by humankind: computers, TVs, radios, cell phones, iPods and BlackBerries, neighbors and pets, timers on appliances, outside traffic and city noises, and more. Certainly music that nurtures and inspires is one valuable stream of sound.

Our fellow travelers on planes are quick to slip on headphones once we have boarded. Music lovers? Or do their headphones help them block out the ambient noise of a crowded plane of strangers?

Following several days of being surrounded with people, I, too, yearn for the isolation of solitude. The pleasure of utter quiet. In quietness, it is possible to engage in meditation and prayer in more meaningful ways.

Do you carve out intervals during the day when you can be still? The admonition "Be still, and know that I am God" (Psalm 46:10 NIV) is a reminder to us to do so. The tumultuous world is ever present. We have only to tune into the news for evidence of that. The most devout believer is not exempt from personal difficulties of life. How can we cultivate spiritual serenity in the midst of the lives we live?

Being spiritually calm is not derived from a lack of troubles. Rather, it comes from our willingness to consistently reflect on God and His ways. God is faithful and will not abandon us. As finite beings, and in the presence of an infinite God, our task may be as simple as "chilling out," and trusting Him.

Today, I will seek a block of time in which I can be still. It may be only 15 minutes, but I'll try to keep the stillness appointment.

How did I find this time with myself and God? Was it a challenge or a simple thing? Why?

Random Act of Self-Care
Reflect on the gift of a loving God.

Whatever satisfies the soul is truth.

—WALT WHITMAN

The story behind the beloved hymn "It Is Well with My Soul" is as memorable as it is heartrending.

Chicago businessman Horatio Spafford, a Christian, had suffered great financial loss in that city's fire of 1871. His family had planned a trip to Europe where they would attend evangelistic meetings then vacation. At the last moment, urgent business prevented Spafford from boarding the ship, but he sent his wife and four daughters. He would join them later.

In a tragic accident at sea, his family's ship was struck and sank in a matter of a few minutes. Among the few survivors was Mrs. Spafford. But the couple lost all four daughters in the accident.

Later, as Spafford made the voyage to join his wife, he viewed the probable site at midsea where his children were tragically lost. In the privacy of his cabin, he wrote "It is well; the will of God be done." Later, he wrote, "It Is Well with My Soul," prompted by his initial words.

What conditions of life create within us a sense of soul-wellness? Some feel at peace and well when life is going well. When adversity is stirred up, we can easily become uneasy and discomfited.

Just as physical exercise gives the body stamina and flexibility, practicing some soul exercises will enhance the soul's vitality. These exercises include keeping the Sabbath and engaging in meaningful worship. Seeking opportunities to laugh. Feeding the soul in ways that are authentic for you, including studying Scripture, praying, ministering to others, being intentionally mindful of God's blessings, and more.

Today, I will explore the habits I have that add to my soul's vitality.

How can I nurture, strengthen, and restore my soul?

I will be intentional in feeding my soul today.

Random Act of Self-Care

For the next week, write down five things for which I am grateful each day.

> Man is so made that when anything fires his soul,
> impossibilities vanish.
>
> —JEAN DE LA FONTAINE

$\mathcal{H}$ave you ever noticed the burst of enthusiasm you feel about a project or venture that ignites your passion?

Your professional role, hobby, family, or church may be the incubator that inspires your project.

Activities are as diverse as the individuals who imagine them. They may run the gamut from transforming your yard with new landscaping, planning a family reunion at the beach, creating a book proposal on a topic dear to your heart, creating an oil painting, or organizing the neighborhood garage sale. Possibilities are endless. Your imagination has been sparked, and you're eager to dig in to the hard work that will make the venture a reality.

Whether you engage in multiple projects simultaneously, or focus solely on one venture at a time, you are invested in the outcome. You don't mind staying up late or doing even tedious work required to make this project happen. Time seems to fly when you are thinking about or doing something connected with this effort.

And, the "red car principle" frequently surfaces. An innovation practitioner, my friend Sylvia observed that when you're interested in buying a red car, you begin to notice red cars everywhere. You can't get away from them. In the midst of your project, you notice connections because suddenly you see the world in terms of that project. You connect dots that were invisible to you before.

Living life devoid of at least one pursuit that ignites our passion is like watching a movie in black and white. Often, color is so much better.

Today, I will reflect on potential projects that would be authentic and fulfilling for me.

I may decide to learn or develop a new skill, or follow up on an idea I had put on the backburner.

My "project" may be framed in terms of meeting the needs of another individual.

I will mine the pages of my journal for ideas that have been in my thinking in recent months. My goal is simply to follow a pursuit that has interest for me.

 Random Act of Self-Care
Try a new recipe.

> The soul, like the body,
> lives by what it feeds on.
> —JOSIAH GILBERT HOLLAND

*I*t takes an intentional act of will to derail our thinking when we're in the worry mode.

A favorite blogger confessed several flaws that she observed in her life, including one related to worry. This woman is a world-class worrier. She knows that about herself, and wrestles with trying to lessen her anxiety. Her self-disclosure prompted me to consider how worry has burrowed into my life too. I resonate with an anonymous author's evaluation of worry: "Worrying is like a rocking chair, it gives you something to do, but it doesn't get you anywhere. "

But oh, how we love to rock!

Happiness and stress management writer Richard Carlson explored how to break the habit of worrying about small things in *Don't Sweat the Small Stuff…and it's all small stuff*. Millions of readers resonate with his description of how we get caught up in minutiae, the small stuff, and never get around to doing what makes us or our loved ones happy.

He advises readers to engage in small acts, such as paying someone a compliment daily, putting a lid on keeping track of who does what around the house, and writing a letter to a friend. All sound soul practices.

Carlson's suggestions are practical and wise.

Today, I will make an effort to pinpoint those areas of my life—small or large—that cause me to be uneasy in spirit.

I will ponder what my worries might teach me.

I will confront in daylight those things that cause me to be sleepless at night. Are there actions that I should or could take that might address those worries? Or can I simply release the thoughts into God's loving hands?

Random Act of Self-Care
Enjoy a cup of tea and a favorite cookie or scone.

The soul is known by its acts.

—ST. THOMAS AQUINAS

We can glean so many wise-living tips by paying attention to people we respect.

You may have someone like Andrea in your circle of friends. When you are in conversation with her, her eyes seldom leave yours, and you know that you have her undivided attention. As she listens, she poses thoughtful questions that stretch you to think about how to respond. She seldom seems in a rush. Almost always, a bright smile radiates from her face. And even if you don't feel particularly upbeat, it's hard not to smile back.

She is a kind soul. You feel fortunate to be included in her wide circle of friends. Sometimes, when my patience is being tried by someone who has interrupted my thinking, I find myself imagining, *How would Andrea respond to this person?* Almost always, my response is more kindly and compassionate when I model Andrea's approach.

My church is known for its boisterous business meetings. Each member is emboldened to share his or her unique thoughts on every issue. Often, emotions become tangled with the issues at hand. Over the years, I have observed a wise brother, Fisher, who seldom joins the discussion until many others have had their say. When he does speak, his tone is always gentle and he makes his points by using self-deprecating humor. He sums up what he has heard, and directs our church family to a course of action that reflects both sides.

At the office and in other group settings, I find helpful the behavior this wise soul has modeled. I silently ask myself, *How would Fisher help us find middle ground?* while in the midst of diverse and far-flung opinions.

My friend Gail consistently welcomes and initiates a conversation with visitors to our church. She does not have a formal mandate for this behavior, but when she spots an unfamiliar face, she makes her way to that individual or family—welcoming smile and hand extended—to greet them. How much easier to stay seated on "her" pew and let someone else take the initiative. Gail is a warm and caring soul who puts herself into the other person's shoes.

Today, I will analyze my soul qualities.

Would others describe me as kind or wise or warm?

Do I possess another sterling soul quality that I might utilize more often?

What might I do differently if I were to emulate a brother or sister who possesses a trait I admire?

🪨 *Random Act of Self-Care*

Write a letter to the author of a good book I've enjoyed and mail it to the publisher.

Mind

It is fascinating . . . to look back . . . and to note the types of concerns, ideas, or actions that were at the top of my mind.

—TREATMENT #37

And then remember the . . .
first word you learned—
the biggest word of all—LOOK.

—ROBERT FULGHUM

What a temptation to coast (or charge!) through daily life, fairly oblivious to people and events unfolding around us.

My left-brain, logical mind races forward with a plan I have for the day—an agenda, a to-do list, and a schedule of appointments. I even have a vision of outcomes and the dialogues with people that I imagine will have happened by the end of the day. And the day hasn't even begun!

Poet David Whyte reminds us, "What you can plan is too small for you to live."

A focus on paying attention to people whose lives intersect ours might mean that we pause, breathe deeply, and refrain from speaking rather than jumping into a conversation. When we do engage, we may try to ask the kind of open-ended questions that pull from others their thoughts and feelings. Looking deeply at faces and others' body language might enable us to pick up on some nuance of pleasure or pain we otherwise might have ignored. Is a word of encouragement or affirmation needed in the life of someone who is in our sphere of influence? Could we choose to encourage with authenticity?

Paying attention means observing the mourning dove nest outside the window and voicing an inner prayer of gratitude for God's creation. Or seeing the deep blue morning glories on a roadside fence when stalled in morning gridlock, and smiling, rather than impatiently fuming about traffic.

King David advised his son Solomon to serve God with a single mind and willing heart. What does a single mind look like? David reminded his son that the Lord "searches every mind, and understands every plan and thought" (1 Chronicles 28:9 NRSV).

Today, I'll be on the lookout for those people or events that I might have overlooked yesterday. And at the end of the day, I'll collect those in a journal entry.

I'll ponder why God allowed my path to cross theirs this particular day.

I'll ask myself how my plans might be too small for my life.

Random Act of Self-Care
Pause and do nothing for five minutes.

The longest road out is
the shortest road home.

—IRISH PROVERB

𝒥ournaling is a means to explore and examine the
inner workings of the mind.

I don't recall my first journal. Rather I remember a series
of five-year diaries—Christmas or birthday gifts—that
invariably frustrated me because the space to write was
so miniscule.

During adolescence and young adult years, I refined
my preference for writing my thoughts down. Journaling
became a habit. Not always in a journal; at times I would
write letters to friends. Some letters I mailed. Others I
simply wrote and kept. My need had been to express my
thoughts to that friend. It was cheap therapy.

In my first teaching position, keeping a journal
was an invaluable tool in my growth as a leader. My
inner-city teaching assignment was a challenge in
crossing cultural barriers. Seasoned co-teachers were
a great resource. But my best resource was my journal.
I recorded hopes, made observations, dreamed about
what I desired to stir up in the classroom, expressed
gnawing fears I had about whether I was really changing
lives for the better or simply being a custodian of a

rowdy group of junior high school kids. There was room on a journal page for all of that.

I looked back over earlier entries, surprised that a fear I had was misplaced, or grateful that a wild idea I had cooked up had come to reality. Successes and failures were equally important in my journaling. I found much to critique in a department chairman's actions. As I sorted through my thoughts about what I viewed as his shortcomings, I imagined how I might do a better job. I didn't stay at the school long enough to realize that dream.

Journaling has been a barometer of how I am growing spiritually, personally, professionally. I have thought more deeply about what's going on in my life, but also about books I'm reading, movies I see, conversations I am a part of—it's all there on the journal page.

Today, I will reflect on my experience in journaling. I will envision what I might like to see journaling become in my life. I'll begin today!

🪨 *Random Act of Self-Care*
Express gratitude to a favorite teacher.

Everyone must row
with the oars he has.
—ENGLISH PROVERB

One of the liberating aspects of deciding to either dabble in journaling, or to begin to avidly record entries every day, is that there are no rules.

Whenever the topic of journaling crops up in casual conversation, some declare themselves as fans of the practice. Others are equally emphatic that they are not journalers. A few may identify themselves as occasional journalers.

I can't think of any other growth practice or leadership tool in which there are no boundaries or have-tos. Perhaps this is what makes journaling appealing to many!

Based on personal experience, I would hold out three guidelines that might enable the novice journaler to experience greater benefits from journaling.

· Establish a regular time frame to focus on capturing a few thoughts. For a daily person, writing every morning or each evening or during a daily commute (on the train, etc.) may work. For a more sporadic journaler, designating an evening or a weekly appointment at the coffee shop may be the ticket.

- Date the entries because the notebooks, bound books, journals, loose pages, or other journal materials accumulate. After a few months, or years, of writing, you may wish to revisit a period of time in your life when you were experiencing a life transition.

- Keep your journal(s) in a secure place. Unless you're writing for publication, you may discover a benefit in knowing that the entries you write are for your eyes only.

There is no hard-and-fast answer to, "How often do I write?" The frequency you make entries is based on personal preference. The frequency may be driven by what's going on in your life.

Because research says it takes 21 to 28 days to establish a habit, if you haven't journaled before, try your unique form of journaling for that time frame.

Today, I'll determine if writing in a journal is for me! Or, I'll think about a new type of journal format I might try.

🔺 *Random Act of Self-Care*

Jot down the names of six characters in a novel I would like to write someday.

No man is so tall that he never need stretch and none
so small that he never need stoop.

—DANISH PROVERB

*T*he human mind is above all else mysterious. Is the mind simply the brain at work? There are numerous questions that only scientists and philosophers can pose, or even attempt to answer.

The mind is an example of the "fearful and wonderful" quality of human life that the psalmist writes about in Psalm 139:14.

I recall my amazement when I first learned about the basic differences between the left and right sides of the brain. Logic versus creativity seemed to explain much about the differences in thinking patterns I had observed in myself and others. Even my elementary understanding of the differences was instructive as I interacted with others.

One mind-stretching habit encouraged by an innovative friend, who is a thinker, is simply to go to a bookstore that features a wide selection of magazines. Select a random number, in advance—say 15. Number the magazines, and when you come to the 15th one, take it to a comfortable chair or reading spot and explore its contents. Chances are, the magazine is not one you would have chosen to read.

As you glance through the articles, what jumps out at you? Within its pages, what are you encountering that is new information? Is there a connection between what you are discovering in this magazine and in any other area of your life? A forced connection, perhaps. What is this magazine teaching you?

The intriguing thing about this exercise is the sheer novelty of exploring a subject or piece of reading matter that is not one you normally select. You may be moving outside your comfort zone. You are certainly stretching your mind.

Today, I will intentionally seek a new experience, talk with someone I don't usually engage, read something outside of my usual habits.

I will pay attention to how I feel when I am pursuing something new for me and journal my reaction.

Random Act of Self-Care
I will make it a point to speak to a stranger I encounter.

There's no need to fear the wind
if your haystacks are tied down.

—IRISH PROVERB

*There are probably as many varieties of journals
as there are the people who write in them.*

Because personalities and preferences vary, journals
are bound to be different. I've learned that some people
keep multiple journals of different types, while others
simply include a variety of content in one book.

There are people who prefer a daily approach to
writing. At times, they even choose to make multiple
entries on the same day. The length of entries varies.
We may find that some days demand a deeper exploration of our lives, or we have more time to write on a
particular day.

One friend writes periodically in her journal, but
every New Year's Day, she blocks out time to reflect
on the past year and to surface personal goals for the
upcoming year.

Another variety of journal is the illustrated journal.
Perhaps creative individuals (such as graphic designers)
would lean more toward this expression. However, an
English teacher friend surprised me when she revealed
that she prefers to keep her journal in an illustration
format.

A journal can have a very specific purpose. A travel journal is an example of this genre. A trip to Croatia, for example, might prompt us to record our thoughts, along with the sights and highlights of our trip.

Many people who awake, aware of a dream they've had during the night, like to record the gist of their dreams. Later they search the dream journal for meaning and even consult books on what various themes mean.

A journal might focus on friendships, nature, prayer, or Scripture. One might collect and devote a journal to quotations. A journaler might choose to write as a means of therapy during a season in her life. Writers often devote a journal specifically as a seedbed of writing ideas. The potential for journaling content is limitless.

Today, I will consider the kind(s) of journaling that I find most appealing.

I'll think back to my first journal and compare it to my current writing.

Random Act of Self-Care
Go browse through a bookstore.

It is a long lane that has no turning.

—ENGLISH PROVERB

❦

*A*re you aware of how you prefer to engage in thinking while participating with others?

A colleague, Beverly, would announce during a group discussion, "I don't know what I think until I hear it come out of my mouth."

I smile, recalling the fine mind Beverly has and the innovative contributions she has made to group thinking. Her analysis about her type of thinking tells me she is an external processor. She tries out ideas as she verbalizes them. She is attentive to others who are part of the discussion. Groups she has been a part of have been lively and unusually creative.

Another co-worker made far fewer verbal contributions to the discussion. Instead, Sheryl made frequent notes. She obviously was interested in the topic, but was more deliberate with her thought process. My assessment of Sheryl's style is that she processes internally. She likes to hear, assimilate, and think through the information on the topic. Then she will speak, and the group will benefit.

Two different minds at work. Two different styles of thinking. Both equally valid in a group discussion.

The wonderful thing about the complex minds that God has gifted us with is that we can stretch our thinking and accommodate others' styles.

Years ago, I noticed that if no one was making a contribution in a group thinking exercise, I could be a catalyst for discussion. Generally, I would preface my comments with, "We're just talking, right?" to take the pressure off of myself for making any deep or profound statements. I discovered that often, others would join in more readily after I had broken the ice.

36

Today, I will think about the opportunities for group discussion that may challenge my mind this very day. I will anticipate how I can make the best contribution, and how I can help others make their best contributions too.

MIND

🪨 *Random Act of Self-Care*

Ride an elevator to the top of a building.

You'll never plough a field by
turning it over in your mind.

—IRISH PROVERB

I often repeat the same two notes in the margins of my journal pages. The labels might read "Idea" or "Action."

In either case, such notes mark the entry and remind me that a creative thought has begun to incubate, or I have discerned that an action needs to be taken.

Both of these categories are particularly valuable if I follow up on them!

Because my memory is less than perfect, I am grateful to be able to peruse pages written months ago and recall that I had considered doing something, or had documented an idea that had cropped up on my radar. There's a certain comfort, I find, by simply recording these somewhat unrelated thoughts on the page. I don't have to depend on my fallible memory to prompt me to action.

It is fascinating, too, to look back, say several years, and to note the types of concerns, ideas, or actions that were at the top of my mind. I am invariably grateful for the growth God has allowed to unfold. I see God's handprints on the direction and shaping of my life. I am reminded that I am not isolated, even if my closest biological family lives hundreds of miles away. God is near and present.

Personal goals and how we plan to make progress on those goals are excellent fodder for a journal entry. As I look back on my journal keeping, I can observe that pages I have created have a hodgepodge quality to them. I have written Scripture in my journal, on the same page with a prayer, a list, a quote from a book I'm reading or at least the name of the book and author, a letter or something I want to communicate to a friend, and so on.

Today, I will ponder the impact of journaling on my personal leadership.

Do I know myself better as a leader because of the journaling habit I've cultivated?

Do I make promises to myself or envision a future dream in my journal? How am I at following through?

🪨 *Random Act of Self-Care*
Reread a favorite book.

The best mirror is an old friend.

—PETER NIVIO ZARLENGA

*M*emory—the process of remembering—is a valuable element of the human mind.

Time may dim a few of the memories that were once vivid and easily recalled, but we can always be grateful for the memories we do have.

Sensory perception is a strong prompter that enables us to remember experiences and people in our lives.

Whenever I get a whiff of Juicy Fruit gum, I recall my grandmother's purse and the chewing gum she would dole out to my sister and me. The smell of chlorine takes me back to fourth grade, when a swimming class was part of my weekly elementary school routine. Do you associate certain aromas with a childhood memory?

Some memories are short-term, like repeating aloud a phone number so that we can remember it long enough to call it. Others are long-term, like the faces of neighbors who lived next door when we started kindergarten.

The search for how the brain organizes memories and where those memories are acquired and stored is the ongoing quest of brain researchers. The human mind is swathed with an element of mystery and complexity.

38

MIND

A woman related a childhood recollection about her father reading to her. She warmly recalled him reading a specific book, which she still loves to read today. Imagine her surprise when she learned that the particular book she associated with that memory was not published until several years after her father's death. In her mind, two memories had merged. Her dear father had, indeed, read to her. Just not that favorite book.

Today, I will reflect on a personal memory from childhood, from adolescence, or from my adult years. What makes that memory particularly vivid?

Having a conversation with a sibling or friend about the memory can deepen its meaning or perhaps cast a new light on the way I remember it.

🝔 *Random Act of Self-Care*
Tell tall tales to a group of children.

> If all pulled in one direction,
> the world would keel over.
>
> —YIDDISH PROVERB

$\mathcal{A}$n intriguing journaling concept is morning pages.

39

Julia Cameron, a writer who writes about creativity, among other subjects, describes morning pages with clarity in her book *The Writing Diet*. The basic idea is to jot down three full pages of whatever is going on in your mind. This is to be done in one sitting. Pen, pencil, or computer takes the lead. No editing, rewriting, or worrying about misspelled words; or whether or not your writing is making perfect sense; or even if it is legible. Simply write with the goal of filling three pages.

Generally, I write my three pages within 30 minutes in the morning. When I stall (that is I finish a thought or a sentence and the next word is slow to appear), I simply pen the word *write* as many times as it takes till a new thought emerges.

Looking back over a week's worth of morning pages often surprises me with the range of subjects I have had on my mind. I may highlight a few that need deeper thought. Because morning pages create a volume of words on paper, I keep a separate spiral notebook devoted to this exercise.

Morning pages are distinctive from a regular journal. The richness and benefit of this type of journaling is that you can go deeply into a topic without censoring yourself. It's like a free-writing or a mind-mapping exercise. Ideas and associations flow freely.

Today, I will experiment with morning pages and see where this practice leads.

🪨 *Random Act of Self-Care*

Skip through a pile of leaves.

He that lets the small things bind him, leaves the
great undone behind him.

—UNKNOWN

*L*ists may be my undoing.

As a lifelong list maker who relishes checking off items
as they are accomplished, I have considered what this
means.

I enjoy the illusion of control as I jot down on paper
the tasks I need to do: the items I should purchase; the
people I should remember with a card; the concerns I
need to pray for; a book someone has recommended
that I read; a telephone call I should make or a prepa-
ration I should begin; the items I should pack for my
upcoming trip.

The words *should* and *need* surface regularly in my
thinking about the items on my lists.

At the end of a day, I *do* wonder how the day might
have unfolded or been different if I had departed from
my list and lived more in the moment. Would I have
followed up on an impulse that was crowded out by my
focus on my list? Would I have been more patient with
an interruption and deepened a relationship? Would
I have allowed myself the pleasure of daydreaming or
taken a trip in my imagination? Would I have spent

a time luxuriating in nature or bought bouquets of hyacinths to feed my soul?

I may never abandon my habit of making lists. Perhaps a winning strategy for me—and maybe you— would be to discover the balance between organizing life (certainly a challenging task!) and experiencing life (surely a delightful journey).

Today, I will reflect on the tension in my life between organizing and rolling with the punches.

How do I respond when changes occur that I had not anticipated?

How often do I take a step back and simply enjoy the moment?

🪨 *Random Act of Self-Care*

Include unexpected vegetables in a floral centerpiece.

40

MIND

To fall down you manage alone,
but it takes friendly hands to get up.

—YIDDISH PROVERB

*G*roup interaction is fascinating.

I manage to do a fair number of things with competence. God has gifted me with skills, abilities, and talents that allow me to be a good student as well as a teacher who enjoys training and learning. He has guided me into a profession that is a good match for the way I am wired.

One of my areas of deep interest is working with teams. I find making a contribution as a member of a group is simultaneously fulfilling and challenging.

The thought that startles me anew nearly every time I engage with a group is that not everybody thinks like I do. This simple concept is one that I have to relearn frequently.

I am also in awe of the power of collaborative thinking. I may see only one solution for a complex problem. Invariably, with teammates at the table with me numerous alternatives become apparent. Often one of the alternatives is clearly superior to my original thinking.

The best collaborative thinking is spurred when everyone is listening as attentively as we can. I have learned on a personal level that I must give up my pet solution, or any idea that I have strong ownership of, in order for the group to wrestle with the concepts and ultimately find the best solution.

Making decisions by consensus is a winning strategy. However, a missionary friend once dramatically threw up her arms and wailed, "But reaching consensus takes all night!" Hers was the voice of experience in reaching a decision by consensus.

Today, I will ponder those areas of my life where I need the collective wisdom or literal help of others.

Do I request help when I need it?
Why or why not?

🔺 *Random Act of Self-Care*
Send a secret pal greeting card.

If you are reluctant to ask the way,
you will be lost.

—MALAYAN PROVERB

I do wonder, *Which gender is more likely to seek God's wisdom when faced with puzzling life issues?*

According to popular wisdom, men resist asking for directions, even when it's clear they are lost. I suspect that characteristic may be equally true for men *and* women.

There's an answer to this conundrum, but it may be beyond human analysis.

Our human minds overflow with preconceptions, expectations, prejudices, assumptions, and opinions. We think we already know what we need or where to find out what we need. But the spiritual life requires that we be open to God's messages—coming from all directions—and that we also be willing to change our minds.

A friend had a traumatic leadership experience that ended in her termination. She endured a lengthy tenure, all the while sensing that her skills were not the best match for the position. She floundered and failed. Once the position ended, she had time to reflect. She, as well as her friends, might ask, "Why didn't she cry out for help?"

God's wisdom is ultimately the only reliable guide when we encounter complex life problems. A family, work, or church-related issue may only have a solution in a deep analysis of the system and relationships within the system. God owns the territory of our minds' deepest thought processes: *Will I look silly for reversing course? Will I still have the respect of those whose respect is important to me if I change direction? Shouldn't I be wise enough and strong enough to tough out this situation?*

The guidance from a loving heavenly Father may be a nudge to confide in a trusted human advisor.

Today, I will dare to think about the issues in my life that I usually avoid.

I will imagine taking action to address the matter that is most like a splinter in my finger. First, I'll seek God's wisdom, and depend on Him for the courage to act.

Random Act of Self-Care
Walk barefoot on the beach.

A teacher is better than two books.

—GERMAN PROVERB

One childhood lesson learned: whatever I pursue in terms of lifework, I want it to be meaningful.

I heard a radio interview once with a popular playwright. While I don't recall his name, a phrase he used to describe his inspiration for a play stuck with me: "the life your father never lived."

That phrase evoked a certain poignancy in my mind. The adult son realized that his father hadn't lived the life he might have wanted to live. The playwright saw in his father a sense of regret and what might have been. A lesson was taught.

My own father worked for the same company for more than 30 years. As a child and teenager, I had a growing awareness that he didn't particularly like his job. The steady income and opportunity for extra income through overtime was the compelling reason my dad stuck it out. That, and the fact that he had a deeply ingrained sense of his role as family provider.

I am grateful for my dad's persistence. I am also grateful for the nudge that his example provided for me. I witnessed the disconnect between his acceptance of a job—where he spent the majority of his waking hours—and his happiness. What would he have done if he had

had the freedom to choose? I'm not totally sure. Not his same job.

I didn't want to grow up and dread going to the office every morning, or have a job like my dad's. I wanted to experience a sense that my job would make a difference in the lives of people. It would be more than just a paycheck for me.

I've thought about that childhood promise I made to myself. And my lifework has materialized into a fulfillment of that promise. I am on a path of teaching and learning, writing and speaking that is fulfilling.

I am reminded of what Eric Liddell said in the movie *Chariots of Fire*, "I believe God made me for a purpose, but He also made me fast. And when I run, I feel His pleasure."

Today, I will consider the difference my life has made on this earth.

When and how in my work do I feel God's pleasure?

Random Act of Self-Care
Stop at the next garage sale or estate sale I pass.

He that conceals his grief finds no remedy for it.
—TURKISH PROVERB

*S*piritual blogs appeal to me because they are similar to reading the journal entries of a fellow believer.

While there are many types and purposes of blogs—the personal blog is a derivative of Web and log—one of my interests focuses on bloggers who write about their spiritual life. I am not a blogger, but have bookmarked several as my favorites.

Blog posts are usually more articulate, graphically appealing, and contain valuable links, more so than any journal entry I might write. And the posts are available for the whole world to read.

I've observed that bloggers take pride in what they write, even if their blog is never read by anyone but them. My heart is usually touched when I read a post where no one has commented or registered any response to the blogger's remarks.

I encountered a Christian chef who artfully blends the topics of spiritual issues and cooking on his blog. His reflections on food, family, and music are unusually well-written. Frequently, I find value in the books he recommends or the musicians he is listening to.

He has battled depression during most of his adult life. He writes openly about the issue on his blog. He expresses gratitude for a wife who supports him when he is going through a bad time, as well as a nurturing family of faith and co-workers.

I am gratified that among his blog readers are those who have experience with depression. There are responses filled with uplifting words that I trust will bring hope into his life. Surely revealing his illness has been a healthy outlet for him. And I feel certain that the empathetic responses minister to his soul.

Today, I will ponder the grief that I seldom share with other human beings.
Are there those with whom sharing a sadness, disappointment, or shame might be helpful?

44

MIND

🗻 *Random Act of Self-Care*
Look through a family photo album, giving thanks—seeking and giving forgiveness where necessary.

The Arrow that has left the bow never returns.

B

*R*ecently, I encountered an ancient spiritual practice called examen, developed by St. Ignatius
Loyola.

Examen is a form of prayer well suited to those of us
who journal or who tend to be reflective thinkers. This
prayer consists of simply taking stock of where we find
the movement of the Spirit in our daily lives. Although
my journaling is usually a morning activity, I find
examen a meaningful end-of-day experience.

Jesus invites us to "abide in me as I abide in you"
(John 15:4 NRSV). At the day's end, we can sit quietly
and gather our thoughts about what has happened
since the sun rose that morning. Some recollections
are happy ones: the laughter of a child, an unexpected
phone call from a friend, the rain after months of
drought. Some recollections are regrets or stressful
thoughts: a critical word spoken in haste, the flat tire
that slowed the journey home, the presence of fire ants
on the lawn.

After listing 10 to 12 things that have made up the
day, good and bad, consider how you have responded or
what attitude you demonstrated. A friend who engages
in this practice says examen is like watching her life

as a movie replaying in her mind. Try to discern your motives, actions, and reactions.

Among many helpful questions worth exploring are:

> In what ways did I notice God in my day?
> When did I feel most energized today?
> When did I fail today?
> When did I feel most alive? Or drained?
> What life patterns do I notice in my day?

Linger over the daily-ness of one day of your life. A natural and appropriate transition is to voice a prayer to God, the Giver of this day of life. You may find yourself unexpectedly grateful. I do. Gratitude segues into a search for forgiveness for the missteps that I've made and wisdom for tomorrow.

Today, I will scroll back over this unique day with particular attention to God's movement in my life.

🪨 *Random Act of Self-Care*
Learn several phrases in another language.

Strength

However long you've been alive, you've faced challenges and experienced life accomplishments. These may be the source of a variety of strengths.

—TREATMENT #53

When spider webs unite, they can tie up a lion.

—ETHIOPIAN PROVERB

*I*t's not our first impulse to rely on others. Our natural tendency is to handle matters ourselves.

Our identity may be grounded in individualism due to nationality or because something else has reinforced the trait. In our professional life, we learn to delegate, but for some of us delegating is counterintuitive.

This week we burrow down more deeply into the element of our strength. We will ponder the dynamic of how to confidently and with trust rely on someone else. Reliance on God is another subject altogether.

Many days I approach life with the attitude that "it's all up to me." I am aware of my gifts and strengths. After all, aren't you supposed to *Soar with Your Strengths* (according to a book of the same name)? I figure, co-workers, fellow leaders, my boss, even friends may not share my level of enthusiasm for the team vision, so I'll just work quietly and diligently and do the job on their behalf.

Being a Lone-Ranger leader has its downside. First of all, it's tiring. And as a leader, I may try to mask my fatigue or stress. I can't let others see how worn-out or close to the breaking point I am. Secondly, I am failing those who emulate me as a model of leadership, because I perpetuate the myth that I am the boss of the team.

46

STRENGTH

A strong leader is available to those who follow, but she doesn't always have to be the PIC (person in charge) or the know-it-all. She trusts that others may be the experts on certain elements of the group task. And she shares leadership, affirming the contributions of others on the team as they wrestle with the task together.

A leader has a strong inner sense, similar to that of the prophet Habakkuk who proclaimed, "God, the Lord, is my strength; he makes my feet like the feet of a deer, and makes me tread upon the heights" (Habakkuk 3:19 NRSV).

Knowing that God makes you as nimble as a deer and able to scale the heights without slipping or fearing the distance above ground you are, what would you attempt for Him? At your heights today, what do you see that may make you dizzy? How will you express your sense of balance and reliance on His strength?

46

Today, I'll identify individuals in my life who may be co-workers or friends or family members who have strengths that I can affirm.

I'll communicate how glad I am for that strength or gift and encourage their use of it.

Maybe I'll discover someone in my life who could use a strength I have. And I won't wait for her to ask. I'll offer it.

Random Act of Self-Care
Do a craft project with a child.

Trust in God, but tie your camel.

—ARABIAN PROVERB

*O*ur physical strength is integrally related to our bodies—those tangible, visible expressions that others see.

Physical fitness, stamina, the appearance of the body—all are signs of our strength and how we are caring for the body God gave us.

The Bible reminds us, "Do you not know that your body is a temple of the Holy Spirit, who is in you, whom you have received from God? You are not your own" (1 Corinthians 6:19 NIV).

Bodies are more than simply what we weigh or the size of our clothing. Health practitioners who study nutrition and body wellness identify several elements of fitness, including:

- *Aerobic Endurance:* how well the heart and lungs work together to supply oxygen to the body during exertion and exercise.

- *Muscular Endurance:* how well the body can hold a particular position over a sustained period of time or how many times the body can repeat a movement.

47

STRENGTH

- *Muscular Strength:* the ability to exert maximum force, such as lifting a weight.

- *Flexibility:* how well the body can move a joint through its full range of motion.

- *Body Composition:* proportion of fat in the body compared to bone and muscle.

In my circle, one friend has successfully reduced her weight and kept it off for several years. Another one has discovered how invigorating walking makes her feel.

Today, I will journal my gratitude for my physical being.

I'll consider the strengths I have, and even mourn some loss of vitality I may experience.

I'll reflect on how I might honor my body through changes I would make in my exercise and nutrition.

Random Act of Self-Care

Plant something in a garden or in a pot.

Nothing to mountaineering,
just a little physical endurance,
a good deal of brains, lots of practice,
and plenty of warm clothing.

—ANNIE SMITH PECK

*C*onsider stewardship of the physical body.

A few years ago, I visited a missionary friend, Lynn, who lives in Shanghai. Each of us anticipated the visit and the adventures we would have during our days together. One of Lynn's objectives was that I would experience life just like a real Chinese person. One of my hopes was that I would live to tell the story.

Following a taxi ride from the airport, she proudly displayed a couple of ramshackle bicycles parked outside her apartment. Bicycles were to be our mode of transportation the next day. She had borrowed one for me. I tried to disguise my surprise, especially since I hadn't ridden a bicycle in recent years.

I survived the miles we rode in Shanghai—"a city of more than 17 million people," Lynn proudly announced to me. My bicycle broke down several times, and always she was quick to connect with one of the many bicycle repairmen who set up shops at the side of the busy roads.

I was mindful of the stamina it takes to live as much of the rest of the world does. For our day of exploring using the most common mode of transportation, I was both exhilarated—the exercise actually felt good—and apprehensive. Larger motorized vehicles added to the challenge. And at times, I literally gasped for breath as I inhaled bus fumes.

My China experience was a vivid reminder of how out of shape I was, and how daily life in China demanded a level of fitness. I returned home with the resolve of making some changes in my level of daily activity.

Today, I will be grateful for the conveniences I take for granted in my daily life.

I will consider the kind of steward I am of my physical body.

Are there changes that I will commit to today?

🔺 *Random Act of Self-Care*

Take a lesson in golf, ballroom dancing, fencing, or other physical activity.

You're blessed when you're content with just who
you are—no more, no less. That's the moment
you find yourselves proud owners of
everything that can't be bought.

—MATTHEW 5:5 (*The Message*)

*S*tress is the first item on the list of forces that sap
our strength and sense of well-being.

Stress rears its head in everyone's life. The term is so
ubiquitous, however, that there may be little agreement
over what stress is. An old 1951 issue of the *British
Medical Journal* read, "Stress in addition to being itself,
was also the cause of itself, and the result of itself."

The thought of public speaking is more stressful to
some of us than the thought of a plane crash. For others,
the opportunity to be in front of a crowd and speak is a
source of exhilaration and delight.

Stress varies from person to person and is no
respecter of position. Even leaders face stress. A
visionary leader's self-care is derailed and energy can be
depleted when one of the following conditions occurs:

Being unable to say no;
    habitually saying yes to every request that
    comes your way; frequently taking on too many
    responsibilities. Setting a few limits and paying

attention to how near you are to reaching the limit is a good self-care practice. A stressed and fatigued leader is of little use to anyone.

Failing at time-management skills

From something as simple as a list, to a dated tickler file, to using daily planners and organizers, resources abound. Practice and commitment in using a particular tool are essential.

Avoiding delegating responsibilities

Delegating takes practice, particularly when I feel that I need to maintain control. There are many ways to implement projects. Trusting a fellow team member to share the load is sensible!

Today, I will look closely at my stress level. Do I feel stressed often?

Are the conditions that cause my stress within my work arena, family, or other context?

Are there steps I know I should take to relieve my stress and to care more for myself?

49

STRENGTH

🔺 *Random Act of Self-Care*
Enjoy a bowl of popcorn.

He who gives to me
teaches me to give.

—DANISH PROVERB

Explore new "rewards" to mark the accomplishment of personal or work-related goals.

When I succeed, my past habit was to treat myself to a banana split or another decadent food treat. Delicious, but counterproductive to a person with a yo-yo weight pattern!

With an eye toward noncaloric "treats," I have discovered some other potential rewards for goal success. In addition to being milestones for accomplishing a goal (such as cleaning out my garage or meeting a writing deadline), they are often celebratory activities that also alleviate stress. A double plus! Consider these:

- Take some time off from the regular workweek. Schedule the time to do something relaxing for yourself: a visit to the botanical gardens, or a museum, or a local coffeehouse for a skinny latte and a session of people watching.

- Buy yourself a bouquet of your favorite flowers and enjoy their beauty.

- See a purely escape movie (or read an escape book). Leave the leadership tomes or Bible studies for another time. Operative word: *escape*!

- Indulge in a bubble bath. This is particularly appropriate if you're habitually a shower person.

- Book a session at a local spa for a professional massage.

- Drop by a nail shop for a "real" pedicure or manicure.

- Consider getting a new hairdo and/or facial.

Today, I will imagine how I would most like to reward myself when I reach a goal I have set my sights on—maybe a weight-loss goal, or a work project.

I will plan how I might choose to celebrate the accomplishment.

50

STRENGTH

🪨 *Random Act of Self-Care*
Go to a playground and enjoy the swing set.

He who is silent means something just the same.

—YIDDISH PROVERB

*I*t is an intriguing, dynamic process by which a group of diverse individuals works together to tackle its team mission.

I have invested in serving with teams in my church and in the workplace. Sometimes I am the leader. Other times, I am one of several members. Always I am amazed by the power of a group of people who take on a task that would overwhelm a single person. Often the end result exceeds anything I could imagine.

Some of the stakeholders at the table spout off ideas more quickly than I can record them in my notes, or even get my mind around. Others assimilate or summarize ideas that members are tossing out. Some members piggyback on the others' ideas, creating new concepts. A few may tend to engage in conversation. Others ask questions and request clarification. A small number may seldom say anything in the group discussion.

Those team members who are not in the habit of verbalizing their ideas are still team members. They have the potential for contributing, but perhaps lack the desire or experience to make direct contributions in the conceptualization stage. Brainstorming and imagining *what if* are not their favorite pastimes.

Until recently, I assumed that if participants didn't offer alternatives or object to the direction the team was going, then they were in agreement. Not so. The adage "Silence means agreement" may not be the norm for every team meeting. Silence may simply mean *I'm not sure what I think right now.* Or, *I need more time to think through the issues of our task.*

As a team leader, I must ask, "What does his or her silence mean?" I can certainly ask a pointed question. I can take the team member's pulse outside the meeting itself. I can stage dialogues or create smaller group opportunities to take advantage of that individual's ideas.

In any case, I am aware that not all silences are equal. And everyone has something going on in their mind. It's my role to help those thoughts move out into the light.

Today, I will reflect on how I came to be involved in my profession.

If I could have a do-over of education or work pursuit, how would my life be different? Would it remain the same?

Do I work better alone or with others? Why? Would I call myself a team player? How?

🪨 *Random Act of Self-Care*
Work a jigsaw puzzle.

The one who is being carried
does not realize
how far the town is.
—NIGERIAN PROVERB

*P*racticing our trust in God by recalling the evidences of His work in our lives is surely a gift.

In the Baptist church of my youth, one hymn was a particular favorite with young and old alike. Whenever our music leader would call out page 231 and lead us in "Count Your Blessings," the sanctuary was visibly brighter. The small crowd sang with joyful certainty. They believed in the wisdom of gratitude.

The simple words of this hymn contain profound truth. Somehow in the midst of deep discouragement, hopelessness, fear, or uncertain times, there is a comfort in considering all that God has done in our lives.

How easy it is to become overwhelmed with the uncertainty of the future. It is a little trickier to consistently remember to express gratitude for what He has already provided in our lives.

The expression of gratitude is a habit of a believer who embraces the wisdom of "Trust in the LORD with all thine heart; and lean not unto thine own understanding. In all thy ways acknowledge him, and he shall direct thy paths" (Proverbs 3:5–6 KJV).

In that same church our faith community practiced a praise time nearly every Sunday morning. Anyone present was encouraged to speak a brief word of testimony about what God had done in his or her life that week. This action was a great training ground, enabling believers to look back and be thankful for His presence, direction, and abundant gifts.

Today, I will make a list—perhaps a page long— of the blessings I count on from a loving Creator God.

Random Act of Self-Care
Pray for church leaders.

52

STRENGTH

He fishes on who catches one.

—FRENCH PROVERB

*C*onsider your strengths; how they developed and how they're expressed.

Imagine that you're in an adult education class and this assignment is given: Create a graphic or word picture of your personal strengths and how you developed those elements. What would your final assignment look like? Consider these categories:

Life lessons

Would your strength assessment include the lessons you've learned about yourself? However long you've been alive, you've faced challenges and experienced life accomplishments. These may be the source of a variety of strengths.

Personal traits:

How would you describe your personal traits and virtues? Are you creative? Would you say you are a spiritual person? How's your sense of humor? Your caring for others?

Personal knowledge

Perhaps your formal education is the deepest source of your knowledge base, but so are the actual

53

STRENGTH

experiences you've had, as is the culture you were born into.

Your talents

What would you include on a talent survey? Do you paint, or sing, or have a decorating flair, or write, or cook well? These are strengths!

Personal stories

A rich source of your identity and strength are the stories that are part of your family culture. These stories are lodged in your mind as experiences. Perhaps many of them are stories you've heard family members tell about relatives you never knew. But the stories reflect your roots and identity.

Spiritual journey

How did your spiritual journey begin? Who shared the Word of God with you? How are you connecting with others who have no relationship with Jesus Christ?

Today, I will consider the strengths I have, and how I use my strengths in service to God.

 Random Act of Self-Care

Buy a bouquet of favorite flowers and put it in my line of sight.

Don't sail out farther than you can row back.

—DANISH PROVERB

*A*m I trying to do too much?

In *The New Why Teams Don't Work*, that deals with teamwork and goals, the authors suggest that a team conduct a "chew-check" periodically "to see that the team isn't biting off more than it can chew."

I resonate with the truth in that concept, particularly on a personal level. I try to practice good time management, but daily life seems to be full of so many opportunities!

Think of these areas of your life, and do a quick assessment of how well you're handling each area:

Friends/Family

I want to spend time with these important people, be involved in their lives, celebrate significant milestones with them, and so on. Are there family members or friends who are particularly needy or who have life situations that are beyond what I can do or be for them? Are there family and friends who reenergize me when I have been around them?

Life goals

These goals are 100 percent dependent on my attention and focus. I decide how committed I am to a life goal that involves time, financial resources, and focus. Pursuing an additional degree, relocating to another state, finding a life partner—each takes time and focus.

Projects due/Commitments

Beyond strictly work projects, are there personal projects that are close to my heart? Redecorating a room, taking an oil painting class, or tutoring a student in English are activities that require time and energy.

Health

Taking care of my body by exercising and eating nutritionally takes a commitment of attention and time. Only I can take initiative in these critical areas.

Today, I will be honest with myself about how much I'm trying to do.

54

STRENGTH

🪨 *Random Act of Self-Care*

Gather some aromatic herbs (rosemary, dill, mint, etc.) and put in a vase on my desk, or near a favorite chair.

To be willing is only half the task.

—ARMENIAN PROVERB

*H*ow many work tasks, or personal tasks, do we undertake and perform without the best tools? Or even without the knowledge that certain tools exist?

I had a recent aha moment in my workplace. My job responsibilities include juggling many schedules necessary to implement various projects. A co-worker observed the paper trail I generated for each project. She suggested using a computer program that I was unaware of. The program would allow me to simply enter actions and dates, and let the computer do the work of sorting according to date, integrating dates across project lines, and more.

She introduced me to a bit of technology ideal for tracking the information I need to stay on top of all the projects. I simply had not known about this software feature.

I would never try to prepare a good cheesecake without a recipe. I genuinely want to do good work, whether it is leading a team, writing an article, or designing a training experience. I want to achieve a good result with my home projects too. Planning an anniversary reception for 100 people, redecorating a room, repairing something that is broken. In each case, making an assessment of the tools that I'll need is imperative.

Consulting with others who have experience in the project is a sound step toward discovering tools. A simple approach such as conducting an Internet search for a project keyword can disclose valuable information and help too.

Our strength as workplace leaders depends on our knowledge of resources and tools. Knowledge of helpful home solutions can enhance our efficiency at home.

Today, I will think about tools that might be helpful to me at work or at home.

What expectations of my role require tools?

Are there tools that would make me a stronger leader?

Random Act of Self-Care
Load a favorite photo as a screen saver on my computer.

Every path has its puddle.

—ENGLISH PROVERB

*H*ow do we react when we encounter disappointments in life?

The disappointment might be a missed job opportunity, a failed relationship, a loved one's death, a health challenge, and so on. A lesson plan for helping people deal with disappointment includes a first step:

Stop. Calm down. Give yourself some time. Things might not seem nearly so bad tomorrow.

An illustration: A college student had studied diligently for an exam. As she took the test, she realized that what she had studied was not quite in sync with what the professor was asking on the exam. When she left the classroom, she knew that it was likely she had failed the exam. She was disappointed, and perhaps a little perturbed with the professor and herself.

However, when she returned to her dorm, she opened the textbook, pulled out her class notes, and began to identify the "answers" that the professor obviously had expected. With a sense of satisfaction, she deepened her knowledge even though the test was past.

Imagine this student's surprise the next day when the professor readministered the same test! He had decided to give the whole class a "second chance."

One student, at least, did much better the second time around and learned something extra from her exam experience.

How fortuitous that her immediate response had been one of *Where did I go wrong?* rather than hot anger or frustration with the professor, the test, or herself. She valued mastering the class material, even if the official test was over. She was looking to the future, and in this case, the future came more quickly than she could have known it would!

Today, I will consider how I have experienced disappointment in the past month.

What was my reaction?

Did I learn a lesson from the disappointment?

How will I respond to the next disappointment?

56

Random Act of Self-Care
Thank God for a challenge I am facing.

STRENGTH

Who begins too much accomplishes little.

—GERMAN PROVERB

*O*s there more than a kernel of truth in the broad accusation that women try to do too much?

We may be married or single, mothers or childless, young or old, professional or unemployed, yet our nature seems to be to nurture others. We often live life around other people's lives, be they spouses, children, parents, or employers.

The result? Escalating busyness, lack of time, and most often, stress.

Does life have to be a merry-go-round that spins us until we fall off? Maybe we simply become accustomed to the dizziness.

Is there another alternative? Possibly.

In *Supermom Has Left the Building,* Judith Edwards explores the myths of superperfection in practical and humorous terms. She offers an encouraging word to moms in particular.

But for those of us who are not mothers (and not likely to become mothers), what is the best path? From experience, these insights seem valuable:

Don't rely on time-saving tips, a Day-Timer, or the latest efficiency manual for the answer to life—as if life has one solution!

Rather than learning to say no, practice saying yes. Yes to what? To those opportunities for involvement and growth and ministry that are uniquely suited to the kind of woman God created you to be. Once you slow down enough to identify what you want to say yes to, then it becomes easier to say no to everything else.

Set aside some time to be still in God's presence, and discover the unique yearnings that God has planted in you.

Today, I will explore my heart's desires in God's presence.

I will consider the unique purposes for which God created me.

I will say yes to what aligns with God's purposes in me, and begin to say no to what does not.

57

🪨 *Random Act of Self-Care*
Take a midday bubble bath.

STRENGTH

Men trip not on mountains,
they stumble on stones.

—CHINESE PROVERB

*O*ften personal strength or vitality is linked to how successful we are in our life pursuits.

When a believer expresses the purpose of her life in general terms such as "I just want to be a good Christian, and serve God," it may be difficult for her to assess whether she's succeeding or not. Goals are a critical element in determining whether you're making progress.

It may be that you resist setting personal goals as too formulaic or too much like work. However, to think personally about life's direction and how you anticipate next year will differ from this year is a good life practice. Being able to express your life direction in terms of what you hope to accomplish, become, create, or discover is a healthy exercise.

And how do you react when what you've surfaced causes you to feel overwhelmed? Or you find yourself procrastinating rather than taking action on your life direction? Or you experience fear about what is required to make your direction a reality?

One approach to addressing a problem, issue, or roadblock to your life direction is to zero in on the cause. Journaling is a great tool for creating the space to "free think" about the parameters of the problem, why the problem has surfaced at this time in your life, and its root cause. You can speculate on causes from A to Z, and heed the intuitive leaps that you'll make as you think deeply about the problem.

Often potential solutions will come to mind, as well as persons who might be able to assist in resolving the problem or issue. Journaling can enable you to tackle some behavior and develop a healthier mind-set and practice.

Today, I will consider what prevents me from pursuing a direction in life that I feel is a nudge from God be it health-related, professional, personal, or relational.

I will listen to God about pathways to solutions He provides for me.

58

🪨 *Random Act of Self-Care*
Unclutter my desk, catchall drawer, or purse.

You may go where you wish,
but you cannot escape yourself.

—NORWEGIAN PROVERB

A critical factor in self-care is knowing when you need to seek the company of others.

For the sake of convenience, we sometimes pigeonhole other people. We have no hidden agenda in classifying others as introverts or extroverts. It's simply a way for us to attach an identifying tag, and it helps us to remember a person more clearly.

A continuum is actually a better "lens" through which to view others. *He seems energized by being around people—today. She is enjoying being alone—today.* People are more complex than we allow them to be.

Theologian Paul Tillich said, "Language has . . . created the word 'loneliness' to express the pain of being alone. And it has created the word 'solitude' to express the glory of being alone."

Are you energized when you're with others, or when you're alone? You may be a hybrid-type of personality who enjoys both time alone and time with others. When you have been alone long enough and need the stimulation and relational perks available only in interaction with others, you're ready for conversation, to laugh and listen, and perhaps play a game.

STRENGTH

Likewise, when you are the center of a family unit, have numerous co-workers, and live a typically busy life in the community and in church, you are wise to pay attention to the signals that *you* need some alone time. You may not have the luxury of a secluded retreat setting, but a time in a room without the rest of the family or a group of peers would be welcomed!

Today, I will be sensitive to my "people quotient." Am I feeling lonely or isolated?

What are my options for relieving that feeling?

Or, am I overly stimulated and need some quality solitude?

Random Act of Self-Care
Read a book when I cannot sleep.

59

STRENGTH

A soft answer turneth away wrath;
but grievous words stir up anger.

—PROVERBS 15:1 (KJV)

*L*istening is an essential aspect of our gift of communication.

How's your strength as a leader? If you are regularly fine-tuning your communication skills, chances are you are growing as leader. It's never too late to begin to develop your skill set!

I once heard a presenter say, "Listening is not simply waiting for your turn to talk." I smiled. I was amused because, though I often appear to be listening, my brain is usually busy framing a response—that I'll deliver when it's my turn.

Listening is an essential aspect of communicating. Genuinely hearing and responding to what the other person is asking is also critical. Often I leave unsaid many thoughts on a topic that I am presenting. When a question arises, my temptation is to deliver an avalanche of additional information, regardless of the question asked.

Proverbs' wisdom directs us to "soft answers." How might I be tempted to answer, if not softly? My voice might take a tone that is strident, harsh, dogmatic, impatient, angry, and know-it-all. Anyone receiving

STRENGTH

an answer in that tone may discount the response immediately. Or, the answer may provoke anger, closing down communication.

A final communication point that I frequently have to relearn is that not everyone has the same thought process. When I am training, consulting, or coaching, I do best when I recognize that it is possible, and even likely, for others to have a different perspective than I have.

Today, I will think more deeply about how I communicate. Who needs me to be a better listener?

How can I zero in on the real issues in conversation and not be distracted by hot-button issues?

🔺 *Random Act of Self-Care*
Invite a friend to share a hot fudge sundae.

The road to a friend's house is never long.

—DANISH PROVERB

*M*obility, geographical distance, careers, and fam ily take their toll on maintaining friendships.

A communication expert at Purdue University, Glenn Sparks, writes, "Making friends is like managing a bank account. You must make investments, and it is never too early to start."

So how's the balance in your bank account?

When I sift through memories of childhood "forever friends," neighborhood cronies, and school chums, I discover that the group is dwindling. I live nearly 900 miles from the community where I attended primary school, high school, and college. I vaguely recall the names of once-familiar neighbors. My bank balance among earliest friends may be down to mere pennies!

Seminary friends, colleagues, and friends from former churches are more vivid in my mind. I actually keep in touch with many of them.

While technology makes keeping in touch easier today, I wonder if the time I spend on the Internet also prevents me from cultivating a real-live neighbor as a new friend?

How do I choose friends today? In a variety of ways including: those with whom I share common interests or hobbies; those I see frequently and with whom common experience is shared; people who laugh at the same things I do; or people with whom I have weathered a life experience.

A boss once bragged that she was forced to play the role of "dream killer." Whenever a team member thought up an idea that was too outrageous, she had the job of pouring cold water on the dream. Friends are at the opposite end of that continuum: they encourage our exploration of *what if.* They affirm the potential they see in us. They applaud from the audience as we give a dream our best.

Today, I will reflect on that group of lapsed friends who were once close and real in my life. I may choose to reconnect with someone in this group to express my warm feelings about how they have added a dimension to my life.

I will be grateful for friends I can reach out and touch today.

🪨 *Random Act of Self-Care*
Offer to provide child care for a friend or neighbor.

He who would leap high must take a long run.

—DANISH PROVERB

Physical vitality, energy, and an optimistic attitude toward life can wane during certain conditions.

What is your signal that your strength is sapped? Or that your reserves are running low?

Jesus was immediately sensitive to the touch of the unclean woman. He demanded to know who had touched Him. He sensed that His personal energy had been depleted (Mark 5:30).

After a week of meetings, juggling deadlines, and/or classroom presentations, you may be suited for a mundane physical task such as edging the yard or weeding the garden. The complexities and pace of the workweek can take their toll on your strength.

If the people you are around during the workweek are noisy, demanding, and stressful, it may be a treat to engage in a solitary activity. You may need to pull aside from contact with others, and engage in an activity that you can perform solo: a walk through the botanical gardens, a couple of hours of reading, or some other soothing activity.

A jam maker I know listens to loud classical music and involves herself in making preserves or jelly as an antidote to people demands.

Conversely, if you have been alone for a period of time, writing, designing, or creating a craft, it may be time for some interaction with family and friends. Take the initiative to invite someone to tea, a meal, or even a trip to the ice-cream shop for some conversation and engaging another adult.

Today, I will take my pulse in terms of how strong I'm feeling. What are the indicators on my dashboard that my strength is waning?

Am I expectantly full or at nearly empty in terms of anticipation and joy for what may unfold today?

Why?

Random Act of Self-Care

Organize my shoes and donate seldom-worn shoes to a charity.

62

STRENGTH

Relationships

Onions have layers, and people do too.

—TREATMENT #63

"You're blessed when you can show people how to
cooperate instead of compete or fight.
That's when you discover who you really are,
and your place in God's family."

—MATTHEW 5:9 (*The Message*)

*I*f you're like me, there are a few people you simply
like more than others.

Your favorite people are in the workplace, in your
neighborhood, and even among family and church
members. There are also individuals who you have just
encountered and about whom you've already formed an
opinion. And not a good one!

You have a warm feeling about Anne, an acquaintance, because she wears fashionable, coordinated out-
fits, and she smells good. You're not as open to Betty,
another acquaintance, because she talks about herself
too much, sports a bad haircut, and frequently inter-
rupts you.

Chances are, you are not going to spend too much
time cultivating a relationship with Betty. She's not as
appealing. She doesn't even understand your jokes.

Being hospitable toward our neighbors may mean
giving people who don't radiate personal charm and
attractiveness—at first glance—a second chance. Hospitality may include practicing the "onion principle."

Onions have layers, and people do too. Peeling back the first layer of superficial appearance, mannerisms, and distracting habits, you may discover a person with whom you can establish a friendship. You open your heart and hands and even your home with grace and a spirit of welcome. The individual has the opportunity to show you her best self. Once you've encountered someone with whom you can exchange personal stories, the relationship deepens.

Today, I will jot down the names of those with whom I can practice hospitality. They may live next door, or be newcomers in the workplace or at church.

How can I express Christlike hospitality?

Random Act of Self-Care
Take a basket of muffins to a neighbor's home.

Jesus said, "Go and do the same."

—LUKE 10: 37 (*The Message*)

*T*here is a divine simplicity, as well as supreme challenge, in the words of Jesus when He told the story of the traveling man who stopped to help.

The familiar gospel story describes a Samaritan traveling the road from Jerusalem to Jericho. His heart is touched when he comes upon one who had been beaten by robbers. The poor fellow lays half-dead by the roadside.

The Samaritan treated him as a neighbor. He administered first aid, took him to a nearby inn, got him comfortably settled, paid the innkeeper for his care, and offered to pay for additional needs should they arise.

Jesus's word to those who heard the story, and to us today, is to demonstrate a similar kind of love in action.

It is unlikely that Jesus will appear to personally coach us through our daily encounters with our neighbors.

Our challenge is to pay attention to those who are part of our lives during this season and in our present geographical place. Those whose lives intersect ours are the men and women whom we are to view as neighbors. And when we observe their need, Jesus would ask us

64

RELATIONSHIPS

to "go and do the same," as modeled by the traveling Samaritan.

Will our actions involve inconveniencing ourselves?
Possibly.

Will being a neighbor cost some of our resources?
Likely.

Will we gain recognition for our efforts?
Probably not.

Will the neighbor express sufficient gratitude?
Probably not.

Will we please Jesus with our expression of hospitality?
Definitely.

> Today, I will consider which of my neighbors is most in need. And I will take steps to be the kind of neighbor who is unafraid to demonstrate the spirit of the Samaritan traveler.

Random Act of Self-Care
Put a flower on someone's pillow (or desk).

64
RELATIONSHIPS

If you see some brother or sister in need
and have the means to do something about it
but turn a cold shoulder and do nothing,
what happens to God's love?
It disappears.
And you made it disappear.

—1 JOHN 3:17 (*The Message*)

I don't want to pass by a neighbor who is hurting, particularly when I have the means to respond.

Are you as uncomfortable as I am when you encounter someone by the side of the road with a hand-lettered sign, clearly legible, with *Will work for food* or a similar message? Do you wait for the traffic light to change, perhaps avoiding eye contact? Those individuals are collectively called panhandlers.

Now I seldom have much cash in my wallet. I have come to rely on an ATM or credit card for personal expenses.

I suspect some of these men and women are genuinely in need. Others have chosen that their "work" will be to occupy a visible place and appeal to whoever happens to pass by.

At times I have felt guilty and stopped to give to the one making the plea. At other times, I have passed by and felt guilty for not digging out my spare change.

I want to be responsive to the needs of my fellow brothers and sisters. My dilemma is knowing what would be an enlightened response.

I have come to believe that my sense of guilt about not responding to the pleas from others is to consider the plight of those I might encounter before I run into them.

Today, I will reflect prayerfully and with thanks-giving to God for the material comfort that I enjoy.

God, what would You direct me to do to alle-viate the pain of those who are jobless, hungry, cold, or sick? Especially those I encounter today.

Help me to not be an instrument of making Your love disappear.

Random Act of Self-Care
Volunteer at church.

Love your neighbor,
even if he plays the trombone.

—YIDDISH PROVERB

*O*ccasionally our minds wander down a path of imagining what life would be like if we had an opportunity for a "redo."

What if we could unsay the words we just declared? Start college again? Choose a different career path? What if we could meet a friend for the first encounter, again? What if we could interview for that new job, again?

The reality of a life redo exists on a continuum of highly unlikely to impossible.

Do you engage in frequent thoughts of how you would change the past if you could? Perhaps not. Living with lingering regrets or second thoughts is not a comfortable place to exist.

Nor is living in the future. *I'll be glad to volunteer for that project or try that new experience when . . .* You fill in the blank:

When I lose 20 pounds . . .

When I become more fluent in Spanish . . .

When I have my car loan paid off . . .

When my kids graduate from high school . . .

RELATIONSHIPS

Delaying an opportunity to embark on a new friendship, or putting God's call on hold when we're feeling a definite nudge is living in the future. And the future is uncertain.

What's left? Now. The present moment. Today. This hour.

Today, I will do my best to release my life issues that are history. Missteps, failures, and regrets will not be my focus for today.

What am I pondering for the future but holding back? Is God nudging me toward fulfilling a call that makes me apprehensive?

I will give God thanks for the clean and unblemished slate of today and all that today holds. May I be open to sharing the joy with both friends and neighbors.

Random Act of Self-Care
Learn to play a musical instrument.

66

RELATIONSHIPS

No one is rich enough to be without a neighbor.

—DANISH PROVERB

A text in Hebrews is clear to readers that we are to be hospitable to strangers because those very strangers may be God's messengers (Hebrews 13:2).

Being friendly toward those we do not know is a stretch for many of us. Being neighborly and thoughtful was what prompted my mother to make an across-the-fence remark to her new neighbor.

Mother spotted the woman out weeding flowers and pruning bushes. Mother drew close enough to her neighbor to be heard, leaned across the fence that separated our yards, and tossed a conversational opening her neighbor's way.

Actually, Mother was usually shy, especially with people she didn't know. And I know it was an act of courage for her to start a conversation with the woman in the adjoining yard, regardless of whose messenger she might be!

Mother called out, "Well, aren't you smart! Getting your yard in such good shape." The neighbor lady nodded, but didn't verbalize a response.

A few days later, Mother learned that the new neighbor's English skills were very basic. In fact, in the course of a conversation between my father and

67

RELATIONSHIPS

the woman's husband, Mother learned she had been terribly misunderstood.

Mom's new neighbor was both puzzled and stung by the words she heard come from my mother's lips. Why was she being labeled a "smart aleck" by her new neighbor?

The miscommunication was eventually sorted out. In fact, my mother befriended the neighbor and, over a period of years, the women shared tomatoes and tulip bulbs from their gardens. A cross-cultural sign of neighborliness.

Today, I will consider my neighbors who may be strangers to me.

How can I take a step toward befriending them? I will be a steward of the grace God has given me.

Random Act of Self-Care

Cook (or purchase) a treat—like a cupcake—to take to a co-worker.

The poor are disliked
even by their neighbors,
but the rich have many friends.

—PROVERBS 14:20 (NRSV)

*P*oor people are often invisible. Or we look past them even when they are our neighbors.

It is easy to ignore those in poverty. They may reside in the same city or live within a few blocks of our homes.

Such a wide chasm of experience insulates us from the poor; those of us who buy books and whatever else we desire, eat out, and own the latest technology. As a member of the middle class, I am unaware of what it's like to be homeless, or to work two to three jobs and still to be hungry.

Our church participates in a lunch ministry. The Christian education members prepare and deliver brown-bag lunches to a local park each week. Other churches in our community implement the program on other days. Our day is Sunday.

The communication network among the homeless, poor, and down-and-out assures that a line of hopeful people are waiting for us to arrive. They notice if we're late. We generally make enough lunches to accommodate all who line up, and occasionally a few will receive a second lunch.

The poor of our city always welcome our simple bag meals. We place them in each outstretched hand with a "God bless you" and, often in return, receive the "God bless you" response of those who receive lunch. When it's my turn to deliver the bags, I try to make eye contact with the poor man or woman and include a smile with the lunch.

Our giving is such a small gesture of love. Surely, shouldn't we do more?

Maybe seeing the poor around us is a start.

Today, I will be grateful for my home, and job, and that I have the opportunity to eat at least two meals.

I will reflect on those who struggle to survive with so much less. I will try to see the poor around me, especially my neighbors.

I will wrestle with my personal response to poverty.

🔺 *Random Act of Self-Care*

Call a homebound friend with a word of encouragement.

> Our greatest glory is not in never falling
> but in rising every time we fall.
> —CONFUCIUS

*A*s I encounter individuals today who are part of a large group we label poor, I wonder what they might be able to teach me?

My mother had 12 brothers and sisters. Her family grew up in a rural community and worked as field hands alongside their father, cultivating their cash crop: tobacco. The work in the fields prevented Mom from attending high school, but she did finally graduate to the kitchen as cook. She declared she did not miss the unending rows of tobacco, the hot sun, and backbreaking work.

As an adult, listening to my mother's stories, I became aware that her family never actually owned the land they farmed. They were sharecroppers. What a startling realization for a "city kid" like myself. Mother's family was poor. That explained her impatience with TV shows that she felt glamorized the poor.

The poverty she experienced within a large, loving family etched some lessons in Mother's mind:

- An appreciation for simple gifts like coffee with real sugar to sweeten it.

- How to make hand-me-down clothes work for the next child in line to receive them.

- The sheer joy of playing outside when there was time for play!

- Reading voraciously because formal education eluded her.

- Losing an adult sister due to complications of childbirth and no medical attention.

- Experiencing the tragic death suffered by a baby sister left alone near an unattended fireplace.

My mother's joyful and exuberant nature and her giving heart grew out of the challenging years of growing up without those things we consider necessities. What can I learn from the poor, particularly those families whose lives intersect with mine, my neighbors?

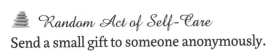

Today, I will rejoice over the material, emotional, and spiritual blessings I have that were not experienced by my Mother.

I will rejoice that poverty didn't embitter her but strengthened her.

And I will look differently at those who lack the material goods I have.

🪨 *Random Act of Self-Care*
Send a small gift to someone anonymously.

"Show me Your ways, O Lord;
teach me Your paths. Lead me in Your truth and
teach me, for You are the God of my salvation;
on You I wait all the day."

—PSALM 25:4–5 (NKJV)

I could notice others around me. I could pay attention to the needs they have, and seek a means to meet that need.

We seldom if ever wake up and greet a new morning with a first thought: *How can I overlook someone today? Or snub someone? Or diminish or slight another human being?*

These behaviors sneak up on us as the hours of the day unfold.

For me the path generally means that I stop paying attention, at least to others. I focus on what kind of impression I am making on those around me. I read faces, and if I feel my words are not understood, I clarify. If my co-workers still appear confused, I elaborate . . . again. Does everyone understand my joke? If not, I'll repeat the punch line.

I have assumed the starring role in my daily life. Co-workers, friends, acquaintances, and family who are on stage with me are my audience.

Could the day become a different kind of experience?

We could put others first. The Apostle Paul wrote a wise word to the church at Corinth when he reminded them that "knowledge puffs up, but love builds up" (1 Corinthians 8:1 NIV).

How can we be more intentional about thinking about others? We can practice. And, when we sense a nudge from God's Spirit, move in that direction.

Today, I will ask that God open my eyes to the people around me, and give me a small spark of care for those I encounter. Then I will fan the spark and see how my day will unfold differently.

Random Act of Self-Care

Say a kind word to a harried person I encounter (possibly in a checkout line).

70

RELATIONSHIPS

No road is long with good company.

—TURKISH PROVERB

*T*he group experience of creating an essential structure for a neighbor was one valued by those who took part.

In the rural United States during the eighteenth and nineteenth centuries, a barn raising was a practical means of creating the first, largest, and most costly structure built by a family who settled in a new area. Even today in some Amish communities, the tradition continues.

During the barn raising, the men would build, the women and girls would provide water and food, the boys would be the runners on the ground providing tools and lumber to the men, and the children would watch and play.

I have never raised a barn. But I recall the energy and the satisfaction that my co-workers and I felt during many consecutive summers when we planned and implemented a weeklong training marathon for missions leaders. Whether we conducted the sessions in the Smoky Mountains or in the great Southwest, bodies as well as minds grew weary after jam-packed days and evenings.

Our staff experienced wonderful worship and learning times together. Yet at the end of the week, everyone yearned to unpack their suitcases in their own homes.

Frequently, participants at the training weeks showed genuine appreciation of some new skill they had developed, a new friend they had made, and a bit of inspiration that ignited their hearts. Somehow all of the hard work of the months leading up to the week, and the week itself, were worth it.

We never raised a literal barn on the grounds at Ridgecrest, North Carolina, or Glorieta, New Mexico. But we collectively raised hope and a desire to grow into better leaders in the minds of those who attended.

Today, I will consider activities I enjoy engaging in with colleagues, friends, church members, or neighbors.

And I will be grateful for those times of feeling my efforts have made a difference.

Random Act of Self-Care
Send a handwritten note of thanks to someone.

Failure is just another way to learn
how to do something right.

—MARIAN WRIGHT EDELMAN

*D*o you belong to the possibly not-so-unique group of women leaders I belong to, whose habit is to feel self-consciousness, particularly when encountering new people?

A stream of self-questioning begins in my head even as I think about entering a room of strangers: *How do I look? Will these folks think I have a contribution to make to the conversation?* While I've abandoned my quest for "cool and hip," I would like to project a professional and fun demeanor.

Strangely, I am seldom "other-conscious." At least not unless I plan to be.

My expectations of myself are high. And I find it simple to compare myself to picture-perfect peers while overlooking others' quirks and flaws. Ironically, I imagine that others are busy totaling up my shortcomings.

My strategy for redirecting my attention? I zero in on one other person in the room. I focus on who she is, what I might learn about that individual's story, or personality, or background. I work on being sincere, holding eye contact, and actively listening to responses.

Often I imagine how I would like someone else in the room to ask me leading questions or bother to get to know me. And then I project that on another person.

I have accepted that, while my self-consciousness is my issue, others may be experiencing their own degrees of self-consciousness too. And if I can be a vehicle for making another person feel more comfortable, valuable, and affirmed, then I may have accomplished my goal of worrying less about how I am coming across. Win-win!

Today, I will be alert to group settings in which newcomers are a part. They may be my neighbors, or co-workers, or church family.

I will be the one who opens the door to get acquainted.

I will dare to listen intently to others.

And I will dare to disclose my unique personality and gifts to others.

Random Act of Self-Care
Go to the spa for a massage.

There is no need like the lack of a friend.

—IRISH PROVERB

*S*hared history among family, neighbors, and church members is a valuable connection among people in relationship with one another.

My Baptist congregation in Birmingham, Alabama, has a rich history and culture. In 1970, hundreds of church members left their comfortable, established church to begin a new church. Beliefs about race painfully separated longtime friends and fellow church members.

Three hundred-plus individuals chose to be a part of a culturally inclusive fellowship and established the community of faith of which I am a part today: Baptist Church of the Covenant. They refer to a particular day in their collective history as "the Sunday that we walked."

Today, many of us who have joined the church were not participants in that early experience. For us, the recollection is a story, told by the "old-timers" who actually made the walk. I used to hear the story more frequently years ago. Today, the early episode has become a significant footnote in a history we celebrate.

Fortunately, in the nearly 40 years since the church split, many additional experiences have unfolded. New traditions have been established. A new building has been erected. We have celebrated growth in the midst of obstacles. We have welcomed new lives, as well as grieved losses together. The lives and stories of many new members have now been woven into the tapestry of our collective story.

Today, I will be grateful for those who preceded me in my church, family, and workplace. They have given me a legacy with the gifts of their energies and the investment of their lives.

I will ponder what kind of legacy I am leaving for those who will follow me in my neighborhood and in the places where I lead.

Random Act of Self-Care
Write a letter to the local newspaper editor.

That day is lost on which one has not laughed.

—FRENCH PROVERB

*D*ifferences are engaging and illuminating.

I grew up in a neighborhood of solid, old brick homes. The homes were occupied by families who were roughly divided between those sending their children to public school and those who enrolled their children in *parochial* school.

As a first-grader, I was not sure what *parochial* meant, but I liked the way the word rolled off my tongue.

During my first several years of elementary school, I came to understand the significance of a parochial school education. It meant first of all that you were Roman Catholic, a strange affiliation for a child with virtually little faith or church understanding. In addition, my parochial school friends, sisters Peggy and Mary Jane, had an entire vocabulary that was enigmatic to me. Words like *missal*, *first Communion day*, *confession*, and *Mass* were slightly mysterious. They wore uniforms to school, in contrast to our eclectic public school attire. They embraced unusual dietary habits such as no meat on Fridays. They observed Lent, and their school was closed several days a school year in honor of a saint.

As an early reader and a lifelong lover of words, however, my most vivid recollection of the chasm between my parochial school friends and me were our lists of spelling words. Both Peggy and Mary Jane, a year apart in school, had weekly lists of immensely more challenging words they were to learn to spell and use. I knew, because I compared their weekly lists to mine, word by word.

I coveted not the fancy white dresses that Peggy and Mary Jane wore to the celebration of their first Communion. But I yearned to be part of a third-grade spelling bee in which words like *mumble* and *thermometer* were part of the mix. I hardly remember my public school list. The words were so simple.

Today, I will be grateful for my introduction to differences between families and neighborhoods that are different than my own.

Though I may suppose everyone experiences life similarly to me, I will allow that not everyone does. And I will be happy for differences in my world.

🪨 *Random Act of Self-Care*
Join a book club at your local library.

74

RELATIONSHIPS

Celebrations have to be made,
troubles come by themselves.
—YIDDISH PROVERB

*C*elebrations are opportunities to draw people together, whether a collective nation is cheering Olympic athletes, or a classroom of children is marking a season.

The Olympics had just ended. The closing celebration was grand in scope and a visual delight for TV viewers. The host country dedicated years of planning, people, resources, and budget to implement an unprecedented spectacle. Undeniably, the Olympics opened and closed with unforgettable celebrations.

As a kindergartner, I recall the indomitable Mrs. Blaney introducing the concept of celebrations to our class of squirmy five-year-olds. In September alone she created visual-interest centers and bulletin boards based on Labor Day and the first day of autumn: celebrations! September also marked the birthdays of a parade of notables from artist Grandma Moses to candy magnate Milton Hershey to folk hero Johnny Appleseed. I believe we also celebrated in the fall a month of focus on Native American peoples.

Through many years of local church involvement, I've experienced healthy and vibrant faith communities that find occasions to celebrate. Causes range from significant to silly. We inaugurated a new pastor with pomp and solemnity (or "staged as coronation!" as some members remarked). Our church also holds an annual talent show that benefits youth; this has provided some memorable untalented moments. Both are celebrations for the body of Christ.

In the workplace, team celebrations of goal accomplishment create a deeper sense of ownership of team purpose and identity.

Are there people you call neighbor who are in need of a celebration? Are you celebrating a personal accomplishment? A goal that your organization or team has reached? Have you adopted a cause or reached a milestone in your life?

Celebrations come in all shapes and sizes. You can share in the celebration of an occasion someone might have overlooked. Peruse Web sites such as http://www.suelebeau.com/months.htm and http://pnyv.org/index.php?id=183 to spark your celebrative imagination!

Today, I will find cause to celebrate! Being alive is such a cause!

🪨 *Random Act of Self-Care*
Go on a picnic, outdoors or indoors.

God promises a safe landing
but not a calm passage.

—BULGARIAN PROVERB

*I*t is challenging to consider all that makes a neighborhood.

During my salaried missionary work as director of a halfway house for women in a metropolitan urban center, I resided in the building as manager. Michigan Baptists had been involved in the ministry for years, and their offices were also located in the building. What a conglomeration of neighbors: women diagnosed with emotional problems, who received daily doses of prescribed medication, and Baptist missionaries. Many stories unfolded beneath that roof.

Women who had lived in the historic four-story building for years were quick to adopt me and offer advice about how to stay safe in our seedy neighborhood. They demonstrated how to clasp my shoulder bag and walk quickly and purposefully down the street. They explained the subtleties of avoiding notorious panhandlers and local derelicts.

Navigating the broader neighborhood of inner-city Detroit was a challenge. The neighborhood within the building became more complicated when we leased the second floor to a group of women residents in a work-release program of the Department of Corrections. Mingling among women neighbors in common areas—the dining hall, the formal Victorian parlor, the basement recreation area—did occur.

My vantage point from an office off the lobby enabled me to coach our residents to be appropriately neighborly, but not intrusive into the lives of our newest residents. The streetwise correctional women hardly needed protecting from us, but they did appreciate having a neutral party (me) to intervene on occasion. The behavior of a few of the long-term residents confused the "prisoners."

Lessons in what makes a neighborhood unfolded under the roof of 2619 Cass Avenue for an inexperienced missionary and for the women who called this place home.

Today, I will explore the kind of neighbor I am to those who live around me, with whom I work, and in my community.

Random Act of Self-Care
Offer to walk a neighbor's dog.

A man shows his character
by what he laughs at.

—GERMAN PROVERB

*W*hat if your neighbors move before you have an opportunity to connect with them?

Finding Forrester is a thoughtful film released about a decade ago. It tells the story of a South Bronx kid who is both athletic and intellectually curious. He yearns to be a writer and appears to have that gift for doing so. A reclusive and crotchety neighbor who enjoyed early fame and success as an author serves as the youth's reluctant mentor.

The inauspicious meeting of the older writer and the boy (caught robbing the apartment of the man, on a dare) creates a launch for their developing relationship.

The likelihood of a friendship emerging between the two fellows seems slim. Yet they do become friends. Differences in age, appearance, style, and station in life become secondary as they share the passion each has for literature. And they are united by being neighbors in the South Bronx. A mentor relationship develops in which the older man ridicules and badgers the youth into refining his writing skills.

I can only imagine a sequel to *Finding Forrester* in some future decade. Perhaps the youth has matured to adulthood, the recipient of the insights and the curmudgeonly kindness of Forrester, the old man. The boy has developed his skills because someone has invested in him, and stretched him, and played the role of advocate in his life. In my sequel, the young man would go on to heights of publishing success, and ultimately be a recorder of the old man's story, perhaps even of his death.

What if their paths had not crossed? What if the robbery had not gone wrong? What if the youth had not somehow endeared himself to the older man? What if the older man had not somehow endeared himself to the younger?

Today, I will imagine being the kind of friend who initiates a relationship with someone in my neighborhood.

O God, keep my antennae up for sensing the person whom You want me to befriend.

🪨 *Random Act of Self-Care*
Enjoy the latest issue of a good magazine with a favorite beverage.

Soul Spa Experience — Group, Retreat, Conference Plans

If you are reading a copy of *Soul Spa: Spiritual Therapy for Women in Leadership*, you may want to facilitate a group experience based on the book. Here are several approaches you will find helpful.

Approach 1: Conduct Two Events

Sponsor a Launch and a Celebration: Host a kickoff event for interested women leaders in your church or other group. Schedule the kickoff for a single evening, afternoon, or even a daylong activity. At this event, provide each woman with a copy of the book or have books for sale. You may want to also have available blank journals (these don't have to be expensive; check for less-expensive items at a discount store). Tell participants that each women will do individual "soul work" for the next 77 days (approximately 11 weeks). Let them know that they are responsible for maintaining a daily journal on what they're learning in terms of their personal self-care.

Soul Spa Event: the Launch

Sites—Choose a room at the church, a member's living room, a lakeside cabin, a community room at an apartment complex, or a nearby retreat center.

Decorating the site—Transform the meeting space into a spalike atmosphere with stations for manicures, pedicures, facials, massages. (If you have personnel or other professionals who can deliver these services, and time to do so, you may want to include one or more of the special services for participants.) Most importantly, provide comfortable chairs to encourage participants to share a cup of tea and conversation. Encourage the women to dress casually, as if going to a spa.

Time frame—If the event is to last all day, consider providing a light lunch and/or refreshments. If those who provide the spa lunch and refreshments wish to share the recipes for the treats, copies of those would enhance the spa experience.

Participants—Invite women leaders who you think might be intrigued with the *Soul Spa* experience. Not all women who attend the introductory event will choose to participate or follow through with the daily self-activity.

During the **Soul Spa**—Enlist a facilitator (a woman leader who has a sense of passion about the value of this experience) to give a brief overview of the potential transformative experience of taking care of those inner parts of yourself. She may share a personal testimony about the critical need to take care of self in order to be effective in all the roles that a woman's life demands. Allow some time for sharing from the participants concerning what they hope to see happening in their own lives, their priority spiritual needs, and so forth.

Ask a second speaker to briefly summarize the use of the *Soul Spa* book and the journal (some participants may be novices at journaling), emphasizing the importance of participants spending an amount of time each day reflecting on her inner vitality and feelings.

Closure—As the spa experience activities wind down, have a time of prayer to lift up the spiritual needs the women have shared. It is possible that some of the participants will want to keep in touch during the upcoming weeks. Encourage sharing email addresses for that purpose. Before the closure of the kickoff meeting, establish the future date (in 11 weeks) when you'll convene to share the results of this intentional journey in self-care.

Soul Spa Event : A Celebration

The celebration event—This coming together, after 11 weeks of personal soul work, could be cast in a spa setting identical to the kickoff event. The schedule could mirror that of the initial event.

The participants—At this event, invite only those women who have been involved in the daily self-care journey.

Some women may have tried and only been partially successful at the experience, and it's fine to include them. Women who have had no contact with the daily self-care process would be at a disadvantage at this event.

The purpose—The celebration is designed to create a time and space for women to celebrate what they have learned during these 11 weeks–new understandings about God's purpose in their lives, priorities that have emerged in their conversations with God about their unique lives, and so forth.

Celebrative closure—Following opportunities to share their unique experiences during these weeks of self-care, provide an opportunity to praise God for His direction in their spiritual growth and community as women. If time allows, consider an activity in which inexpensive flip-flops (spa shoes) are decorated and signed by each participant. These may be symbolic reminders for the women to take home. They'll recall the experience they have had together whenever they see the flip-flops. Consider giving each woman a symbol of growth as a parting gift, for example a bulb she might plant and recall this spa experience or a green plant to which she will give regular care and that will remind her of the regular self-care that she must attend to for her own spiritual vitality.

Approach 2: Weekly Meetings

If the women leaders in your church lean more toward a weekly meeting format, the *Soul Spa* book will easily accommodate this schedule.

Gather potential participants—Publicize in advance the opportunity for women who want to be a part of a *Soul Spa* experience. Conduct an informational meeting for any women who are curious and intrigued by the concept. Make books available at that meeting, or give out WMU's 1-800-968-7301 number so participants may order *Soul Spa: Spiritual Therapy for Women in Leadership* (New Hope product number N094150).

Establish a regular meeting time—Among the women who are willing to commit to the *Soul Spa* experience, establish a time for the meeting—an evening, a Sunday afternoon, or some other time. The time frame necessary to complete all sections of the book will be 11 weeks. Meeting at the church or at the home of a participant is feasible. Allow between one to two hours for each meeting. If a large number of women are interested, consider forming more than one group. Maximum group size would be between 15 to 20 women.

Refreshments may be a part of the experience. It is desirable for a spa covenant to be established at this first meeting including such understandings as:

- I will make attendance at the weekly meeting a priority for the next 11 weeks.

- I will be faithful in my daily interaction with the daily entry and the journal prompt.

- I will be prayerful about concerns shared in the context of this small-group experience.

- I will keep the confidences shared in this group.

Add others as needed to fit your group.

At the weekly meeting—It is important to designate a facilitator for the meeting, though this role can rotate among women members. The facilitator role is to open and conclude the meeting promptly, welcome the women who have gathered, ask God's guidance as the group considers spiritual growth and development. The facilitator role may be a revolving function. The consideration of what you have been reflecting on during a given week is the central topic of discussion.

Weeks 1–2: Focus on the heart
Weeks 3–5: Focus on the soul
Weeks 6–7: Focus on the mind
Weeks 8–9: Focus on the strength
Weeks 10–11: Focus on relationships

Facilitator's role—Though each small group will develop its own rhythm and pace for debriefing, one way to allow for maximum opportunities for input from the members is to begin by reminding the group of the overarching topic for the week: the heart, soul, and so forth. Having the key verse (Mark 12:30) posted visibly would be helpful in tying consideration of our lives to the Scripture. Ask open-ended questions such as:

- *According to your journal, or memory, what was the highlight of your experiences this week? Why?*

- *What was hard for you to write about this week? Why?*

- *Which of the daily quotes was meaningful to you this week? Why?*

Give the participants a few minutes to leaf through their journals. Then ask,

- *Did you surprise yourself this week in your reflecting and writing? How?*

- *Did you engage in any of the daily activity suggestions? Tell us a story about that. How about the random acts of self-care?*

- *What did God reveal to you this week?*

- *How will life be different next week?*

Approach 3: Monthly Meetings

If your women wish to meet on a monthly basis, the model for that schedule is a slight modification of the weekly meeting approach.

Implement the "Gather potential participants" step (from the weekly approach.)

Schedule—Decide on a schedule of three upcoming dates for a monthly gathering. Allow one and a half to two hours for a good debriefing. If the group is large, consider dividing into two groups, each with its own facilitator.

First monthly meeting—Designate a group facilitator who can guide each meeting. The role can be handled by more than one person if you desire. The facilitator role is to open and conclude the meeting promptly, welcome the women who have gathered, and ask God's guidance as the group considers spiritual growth and development. She moderates the discussion of what the women have experienced during the previous month as they have used the *Soul Spa* book to guide their reflections.

Facilitator's role—Each small group will develop its own rhythm and pace for debriefing. Ideally the facilitator is comfortable posing open-ended questions and guiding the discussion that ensues. Consider these discussion starters:

- *According to your journal, or memory, what was the highlight of your experiences during the past month? Why?*

- *Was there a particular entry that was hard for you to write about? Why?*

- *Which of the daily quotes was especially meaningful? Why?*

Give the participants a few minutes to leaf through their journals. Then ask,

- *Did you surprise yourself in your reflecting and writing? How?* (Consider asking the women to respond to this question with a partner, rather than the whole group.)

- *Did you engage in any of the daily activity suggestions? Tell us a story about that. How about the random acts of self-care?*

- *What did God reveal to you during this past month?*

- *How will life be different next month?*

77 Plus 33 More Random Acts of Self-Care

Note to the Reader: Why would you choose to invest time or energy to engage in any of these self-care acts? Consider that doing something out of your routine might prompt you to view your life and God's presence in your life differently than you're accustomed to doing. You may encounter an unexpected blessing or an aha moment of learning. Perhaps you'll only do one or a few of these self-care acts. And that's OK too!

Index

Research the ideal vacation on the Internet. (39)

Listen to a child tell a story. (41)

Take a canoe trip or a ferryboat ride. (43)

Take a Sunday afternoon nap. (47)

Share something with a friend that has surprised, touched, or
inspired me. (49)

Invite friends over for a game night. (51)

Take a walk in the rain, or sunshine, or, if there's snow, make a
snow angel. (53)

Make a batch of jelly or jam or preserves. (55)

Wear a hat to church. (57)

Play a game with a child (such as Uno, Candyland,
or Go Fish). (59)

Go to the beach and watch the waves or to the park and watch
wind sway the trees. (61)

Enjoy a few sprigs of lilac, forsythia, or cherry blossoms. (63)

Reflect on the gift of a loving God. (65)

For the next week, write down five things for which I am
grateful each day. (67)

Try a new recipe. (69)

Enjoy a cup of tea and a favorite cookie or scone. (71)

Write a letter to the author of a good book I've enjoyed and
mail it to the publisher. (73)

Pause and do nothing for five minutes. (77)

Express gratitude to a favorite teacher. (79)

Jot down the names of six characters in a novel I would like to
write someday. (81)

I will make it a point to speak to a stranger I encounter. (83)

Go browse through a bookstore. (85)

Ride an elevator to the top of a building. (87)

Reread a favorite book. (89)

Tell tall tales to a group of children. (91)

Skip through a pile of leaves. (93)

Include unexpected vegetables in a floral centerpiece. (95)

Send a secret pal greeting card. (97)

Walk barefoot on the beach. (99)

Stop at the next garage sale or estate sale I pass. (101)

Look through a family photo album, giving thanks, seeking and
giving forgiveness where necessary. (103)

Learn several phrases in another language. (105)

Do a craft project with a child. (109)

Plant something in a garden or in a pot. (111)

Take a lesson in golf, ballroom dancing, fencing, or
other physical activity. (113)

Enjoy a bowl of popcorn. (115)

Go to a playground and enjoy the swing set. (117)

Work a jigsaw puzzle. (119)

Pray for church leaders. (121)

Buy a bouquet of favorite flowers and put it in my
line of sight. (123)

Gather some aromatic herbs (rosemary, dill, mint, etc.) and
put in a vase on my desk, or near a favorite chair. (125)

Load a favorite photo as a screensaver on my computer. (127)

Thank God for a challenge I am facing. (129)

Take a midday bubble bath. (131)

Unclutter my desk, catchall drawer, or purse. (133)

Read a book when I cannot sleep. (135)

Invite a friend to share a hot fudge sundae. (137)

Offer to provide child care for a friend or neighbor. (139)

Organize my shoes and donate seldom-worn
shoes to a charity. (141)

Take a basket of muffins to a neighbor's home. (145)

Put a flower on someone's pillow (or desk). (147)

Volunteer at church. (149)

Learn to play a musical instrument. (151)

Cook (or purchase) a treat—like a cupcake—to
take to a co-worker. (153)

Call a homebound friend with a word of encouragement. (155)

Send a small gift to someone anonymously. (157)

Say a kind word to a harried person I encounter (possibly in a
checkout line). (159)

Send a handwritten note of thanks to someone. (161)

Go to the spa for a massage. (163)

Write a letter to the local newspaper editor. (165)

Join a book club at your local library. (167)

Go on a picnic, outdoors or indoors. (169)

Offer to walk a neighbor's dog. (171)

Enjoy the latest issue of a good magazine with a
favorite beverage. (173)

33 More Random Acts of Self-Care

Put a wreath on the front door when it's not Christmas.

Write a note to a friend you haven't seen in a while.

Watch a sunrise, sunset, or moonrise.

Reflect on the gift of good health.

Invite a preschooler to a playground or park for a play time.

Treat yourself to a pedicure.

Take a plate of cookies or cupcakes to my local police

Take a plate of cookies or cupcakes to my local fire station to say
thanks for what they do.

Play a favorite song on the piano (or CD, iPod, etc.).

Start a journal. If I already journal, I'll consider exploring another
   kind of journal: gratitude, prayer, favorite Scriptures,
   illustrated journal, etc.

Play with my cat (or dog, or bird, etc.).

Take a walk outside.

Call a homebound friend with a word of encouragement.

View an old, favorite movie.

Read selections from a book of poetry.

Visit a local art museum or gallery.

Spend 15 minutes swinging in a front porch swing.

Take a midday bubble bath.

Complete a crossword—or Sudoku—puzzle.

Memorize the US state capitals.

Go to the newsstand and read a magazine you've
   never read before.

Tuck a note into a lunchbox or briefcase.

Send a small gift to someone anonymously.

Put a wreath on your front door when it's not Christmas.

Take an architectural tour.

Watch butterflies, ladybugs, or dragonflies

Sit in an open, sun-filled window and feel the breeze.

Sit by a public fountain.

Have a homemade oatmeal facial with cucumber slices
   for my eyes.

Sit under a tree.

Blow bubbles.

Watch fireworks.

Rest by the warmth of a fireplace or campfire.

New Hope® Publishers is a division of WMU®, an international organization that challenges Christian believers to understand and be radically involved in God's mission. For more information about WMU, go to www.wmu.com. More information about New Hope Publishers may be found at www.newhopepublishers .com. New Hope books may be purchased at your local bookstore.

If you've been blessed through this book, we would like to hear your story. The publisher and author welcome your comments and suggestions at:

newhopereader@wmu.org

Also from

New Hope

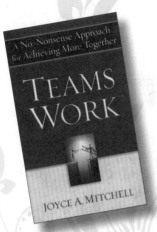

Teams Work
A No-Nonsense Approach for Achieving More Together
Joyce A. Mitchell
ISBN-10: 1-59669-211-1
ISBN-13: 978-1-59669-211-4

5 Leadership Essentials for Women
Developing Your Ability to Make Things Happen
Linda Clark
ISBN 10: 1-56309-842-3
ISBN 13: 978-1-56309-842-0

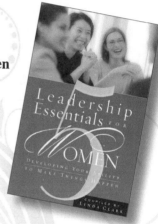

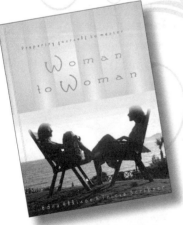

Woman to Woman
Preparing Yourself to Mentor
Edna Ellison and Tricia Scribner
ISBN-10: 1-56309-949-7
ISBN-13: 978-1-56309-949-6

Available in bookstores everywhere

NEW HOPE
PUBLISHERS

For information about these books or any New Hope product,
visit www.newhopepublishers.com.